privity of contract

a practitioner's guide to The Landlord and Tenant (Covenants) Act 1995

by

for The College of Law:
Alan Riley
Philip Rogers

for Titmuss Sainer Dechert:
Steven Fogel
Emma Slessenger

for Hillier Parker:
Alan Patterson

The College of Law, Braboeuf Manor, St Catherines, Guildford, Surrey GU3 1HA

ISBN 0 905835 59 X

Printed in Great Britain by Rexam Digital Imaging Limited, Reading

table of
contents

foreword

The Landlord and Tenant (Covenants) Act 1995 is expected to come into force on 1 January 1996. It will abolish privity of contract for new leases, and do many other things besides. Although the Act is the product of a long campaign by tenants for the abolition of privity, and was preceded by a Law Commission report, it occupied the time of Parliament for no more than a few hours, and its passage through both Houses of Parliament was completed in no more than a few weeks. This haste has meant that the Act has lacked detailed public discussion of its implications. This book remedies that deficiency.

The Act will affect all property dealings. Lawyers, valuers, investors and consumers of property will all need to know how the Act will affect them and their practices. The contributors to this book include some of those who played a key role in advising behind the scenes on the policy of the Act, and indeed on the detailed drafting of some of its provisions.

They explain lucidly and simply what the Act does and what changes it has made. They discuss the practical implications of the changes, and suggest both drafting responses, and responses in working practices to cope with these changes. The multi-disciplinary team of contributors also enables the valuation implications of the Act to be covered.

The book also includes the Act itself.

It is rare for a new Act to receive such thoughtful and comprehensive examination even before it is brought into force. The property profession has every reason to be grateful.

Kim Lewison QC
Falcon Chambers

introduction

1 January 1996 is a date destined to become familiar to lawyers and other professionals involved in property transactions as the date upon which the Landlord and Tenant (Covenants) Act 1995 becomes operative. After more than ten years campaigning, tenants have finally persuaded Parliament to change the rules on privity of contract in relation to leases. For leases granted on or after this date, the Act introduces a completely new regime of covenant liability. But it is not just 'new' leases which are affected: certain provisions of the Act apply to all leases, whenever made.

As a result of these significant changes it is essential for all practitioners to become familiar with the varied (and sometimes innovative) provisions of the Act and be ready to advise their clients upon the implications of the changes. The aim of this book is to enable the reader to do this by providing:

▷a comprehensive guide to the new statutory framework written in an easy to understand manner by experienced COLLEGE OF LAW lecturers, specialising in landlord and tenant matters; and solicitors at the leading firm of solicitors TITMUSS SAINER DECHERT, who advised the British

Retail Consortium on the passage of the Bill through Parliament;

▷ expert professional advice;

▷ an insight by **HILLIER PARKER** into the market view of the changes and their impact on lease negotiations.

Unless otherwise stated, statutory references in this booklet are references to the Landlord and Tenant (Covenants) Act 1995.

preliminary matters

1.1 THE MAIN CHANGES, AT A GLANCE

For 'new' leases:

- abolition of the concept of privity of contract (but note the authorised guarantee provisions, see chapter 3);
- amendment of section 19(1) of the Landlord and Tenant Act 1927 (the 1927 Act) to allow the parties to the lease to specify in advance the conditions which must be satisfied before the landlord will agree to an assignment (see chapter 4);
- on the sale of the reversion, the outgoing landlord may apply to the tenant to be released from the landlord's obligations (see chapter 2).

For all leases:

- if a landlord wishes to pursue a former tenant (or his guarantor) for what the Act calls a 'fixed charge' (e.g. rent), the landlord must serve notice of the claim within 6 months of the current tenant's default (see chapter 5);
- where a former tenant (or his guarantor) is served with notice of the current tenant's non-payment of a 'fixed charge', he can, on making full payment, call for an overriding lease from the landlord (see chapter 6);
- former tenants will not be liable for any increased liability resulting from certain lease variations which occur after assignment (see chapter 7).

1.2 WHAT IS A 'NEW' LEASE?

Section 1 of the Act defines a 'new' lease as one granted on or after the date the Act comes into force (1 January 1996). However, there are exceptions which exclude from the definition those leases granted on or after 1 January 1996 pursuant to:

- an agreement for lease;
- an option for a lease;
- a court order

made before that date.

There are several implications of the definition of a new lease.

(i)   A renewal lease under Part II of the Landlord and Tenant Act 1954 (the 1954 Act) ordered or agreed on or after 1 January 1996 will be a new lease. This will often mean that, while under the existing lease (granted before 1 January 1996), the original tenant was liable for the entire duration of the term through privity of contract, this will not apply to the renewal lease. This change is one of the circumstances to which the court must have regard in fixing the rent and other terms of the new lease under amended sections 34 and 35 of the 1954 Act (and see the *O'May* case, below).

(ii) Section 1(5) of the Act preserves the existing rule that certain lease variations (e.g. to extend the term: *Baker v Merckel* [1960] 1 QB 657) operate as a surrender and regrant. Landlords will need to be aware of the fact that if they agree to such a variation on or after 1 January 1996 the new privity rules will be introduced and former tenants and their guarantors will be completely released.

(iii) For the position on the grant of an overriding lease see 6.4 below.

(iv) For the position on forfeiture where relief is obtained by someone other than the tenant, see the *practitioner's view* below.

(v)   For the position following disclaimer, see 3.2.3 below.

1.3 ANTI-AVOIDANCE

There can be no contracting out of the Act (s 25). Any agreement relating to a tenancy is void to the extent that it:

- purports to exclude, modify or otherwise frustrate the provisions of the Act; or
- provides for:
  - the termination or surrender of the tenancy; or
  - the imposition of any penalty, disability or liability

  in the event of the operation of any provision of the Act.

A PRACTITIONER'S VIEW

▷Both landlords and tenants may wish to consider delaying entering into leases until the Act is in force. This will enable landlords to take advantage of the new power to specify in advance the conditions which must be satisfied before consent to assignment will be forthcoming (see chapter 4), and tenants to take advantage of the new privity rules (see 2.1).

▷As noted at 1.2, on the renewal of a lease under the 1954 Act, the court must have regard to the effect of the Act upon the terms of the renewal lease. If the lease being renewed was granted before 1 January 1996, then notwithstanding the effect of *O'May v City of London Real Property Co Ltd* [1983] 2 AC 726, landlords may seek to alter the terms of the alienation covenant to give them greater control over assignments and thereby balance the effect of the loss of privity of contract.

▷Where the court orders a renewal lease before 1 January 1996 (and the lease is therefore subject to the old privity regime), dissatisfied tenants should not overlook the right in section 36(2) of the 1954 Act to apply for revocation of the order within 14 days.

▷Only where a renewal lease is granted pursuant to a binding agreement between the parties or a court order made before 1 January 1996 will the lease be subject to the old privity regime. If the parties reach a (non-binding) agreement before that date but completion is delayed, the renewal lease will be subject to the new regime. In such cases landlords will want to renegotiate the terms. Alternatively, the possibility of delay can be dealt with by agreeing terms which will vary depending upon when the lease is granted.

▷ Where a lease is forfeited and a person other than the current tenant successfully applies for relief after the Act has come into force, the resulting lease will be a new lease, even if the forfeited lease was an old one. Landlords may want to resist the grant of relief in such circumstances as the lease would still have an old-style alienation covenant but new-style tenant release. Alternatively, landlords may seek to persuade the court that relief should only be granted on terms that the alienation covenant is varied.

▷ Although not required to do so by the Act, practitioners will assist their successors and their clients by clearly identifying leases falling within the exceptional cases set out in 1.2, preferably by inserting a brief but prominent statement into the lease.

▷ On all dealings involving leases granted on or after 1 January 1996 practitioners must be alert to the possibility that the leases may be subject to the old privity regime. Preliminary enquiries about preceding agreements for lease, options and court orders may be required.

▷ The position at rent review of an existing lease (assuming the review date is after the commencement of the Act) is not entirely satisfactory. The hypothetical lease is usually one which is notionally granted at the review date and will, therefore, be a new lease. In such a situation it is arguable that a hypothetical tenant might be prepared to pay a higher rent for the benefit of a lease granted under the new regime where there is no continuing liability after assignment. This is particularly so if the hypothetical lease incorporates the alienation clause contained in the actual lease (as would normally be the case), rather than one which allows the landlord a greater degree of control over assignments, as permitted in new leases (see chapter 4). This may lead to a two tier market in which tenants under existing leases end up paying higher rents for something they have not got. Tenants may try to argue that any court invited to construe the operation of the lease would apply a 'presumption of reality' and strive for an interpretation of the clause which did not result in an inflated rent. One possibility might be for the court to find that the hypothetical lease is to be regarded as granted (as is indeed the case in reality) pursuant to the lease which contains the rent review. It would be as if that lease were an agreement for the grant of the hypothetical lease so that the hypothetical lease is an old lease under section 1. Many practitioners would regard this approach as consistent with the robustness demonstrated in *Broadgate Square plc v Lehman Brothers Ltd* [1995] 01 EG 111. See Precedent 1 (page 104) for a drafting suggestion for leases granted before the Act comes into force.

Case law may be expected on this issue.

the new privity regime

For leases granted before 1 January 1996 there is no change to the existing rules on privity of contract. The original parties remain liable on their covenants throughout the term despite any disposition of their interests. Readers who require a description of the existing rules are referred to one of the standard works on landlord and tenant law for a detailed consideration of them (e.g. *The Landlord and Tenant Factbook* written by Titmuss Sainer Dechert, and published by Gee Publishing).

However, for leases granted on or after 1 January 1996 there are significant and far-reaching changes. For a more detailed consideration of the rules relating to the release and transmission of covenants see chapter 8.

2.1 POSITION OF OUTGOING TENANT ON ASSIGNMENT OF A NEW LEASE (TENANT'S RELEASE)

The basic rule is that a tenant under a new lease is only liable for breaches of covenant committed whilst the lease is vested in him. Thus, on assignment of the whole of the premises comprised in a lease, the assignor is released from all the tenant covenants of the tenancy (and ceases to be entitled to the benefit of the landlord's covenants)(s 5(1)). For the position on an assignment of just part of the demised premises see chapter 8.

2.1.1 Exceptional extensions of liability

However, while the general rule is that a tenant can no longer be made liable for breaches occurring after he has assigned his interest, there are a

few exceptional cases in which a tenant's liability may extend beyond the
date of an assignment by him.

- On assignment, an outgoing tenant can be required by his landlord to
  guarantee performance of the tenant covenants by his immediate
  assignee. This is known as an 'authorised guarantee agreement' (AGA)
  (see chapter 3).

- If the immediate assignee's liquidator or trustee in bankruptcy disclaims
  the lease and the assignor, under his AGA, is required to take a fresh
  lease, then on assignment of that lease he can again be required to
  guarantee the performance of his immediate assignee under the fresh
  lease.

- If a former tenant calls for an overriding lease (see chapter 6), then on
  assignment of that lease he may (if the overriding lease is a new lease)
  be required to guarantee the performance of his immediate assignee.

- On an excluded assignment (see below).

2.1.2 Excluded assignments

Assignments in breach of covenant or by operation of law (e.g. on the death
or bankruptcy of a tenant) are defined by section 11 of the Act as 'excluded
assignments'. The effect of section 11 is that such an assignment will not
release the assignor who will remain liable jointly and severally with the
assignee until the next assignment which is not an excluded assignment takes
place. However, on that later assignment, both the former tenant and the
current tenant may be required to enter into an AGA with the landlord
(s 16(6)). For example, T assigns in breach of covenant to A1. Both T and
A1 are liable on the lease covenants. A1 assigns to A2 with consent. T and
A1 are released from liability but L may require an AGA from both of them
to guarantee performance of the tenant covenants by A2. When A2 assigns
with consent to A3, both T and A1 are released from their AGAs, but A2
may be required to guarantee A3.

2.2 Position of incoming tenant on assignment of a new lease

As from the date of assignment, an assignee becomes bound by the tenant covenants in the lease except to the extent that immediately before the assignment they did not bind the assignor (s 3). One slight change for new leases is that an assignee will be liable on all such covenants in the lease whether or not they 'touch and concern' the land. However, an assignee is not liable on a covenant which is expressed to be personal (s 3(6)). Similarly, the assignee becomes entitled to the benefit of the landlord's covenants in the lease.

2.3 POSITION OF OUTGOING LANDLORD ON ASSIGNMENT OF THE REVERSION OF A NEW LEASE (LANDLORD'S RELEASE)

On an assignment of the reversion there is no automatic release for the outgoing landlord from his obligations under the lease. The release does not mirror the tenant's release by operating automatically. This is because, while the tenant usually assigns after obtaining the landlord's consent, a lease does not normally give the tenant any control over the identity of his landlord.

Instead, sections 6 and 8 of the Act provide a procedure whereby the assigning landlord can apply to the tenant to be released from his obligations under the lease. Either before, or within four weeks of the assignment, the outgoing landlord may serve a notice (in a prescribed form) on the tenant (or each tenant if the premises are in multi-occupation) informing him of:

- the proposed assignment or (as the case may be) the fact that the assignment has taken place, and
- the request for the covenant(s) to be released.

Where such a notice has been served, the covenant(s) will be released to the extent mentioned in the landlord's notice unless, within four weeks of service, the tenant (or any of them) objects by serving a written notice on the landlord. Whether a tenant objects will depend on many factors and in particular the extent of the landlord's obligations. If the lease contains onerous covenants on the landlord's part, such as the provision of services, the tenant may wish to be assured that any new landlord will be of sufficient financial standing and reputation to meet the obligations. If a notice of objection is served by the tenant(s), the landlord may apply to the county court for a declaration that it is reasonable for the covenant to be released.

If the tenant does not object to the landlord's release he can either do nothing, in which case the landlord will be released four weeks later, or, he may give written consent within the four weeks under section 8(2)(c).

Any release from a covenant under these provisions is regarded as occurring at the time when the assignment in question takes place.

If a landlord does not obtain a release, the outgoing landlord remains jointly and severally liable with the assignee. However, section 7 gives the former landlord another opportunity to apply for release when the new landlord disposes of the reversion (provided it is not an excluded assignment; see 2.3.1 below).

Where the landlord is not released, he remains entitled to the benefit of the tenant covenants in the lease equally with the new landlord. The theoretical possibility of parallel claims from the old and the new landlord may be one reason why a tenant will consent to the release of the old landlord.

If a landlord is released under these provisions, he ceases to be entitled to the benefit of the tenant covenants in the lease as from the date of the assignment (s 6(2)(b)). A similar rule applies where a landlord has been released from a covenant on the assignment of part only of the reversion (s 6(3)). The former landlord remains entitled to sue for a breach of covenant committed before the date of the assignment (s 23(1)), although this right can be assigned to his successor (s 23(2)). On an assignment of a reversion where there are arrears, the seller and buyer will need to decide whether to leave the seller to sue or to assign the right to sue to the buyer. As section 23(1) reverses the previous position for new leases only, practitioners will need to exercise particular care with properties subject to a mixture of old and new leases.

2.3.1 Excluded assignments

An assignment of the reversion in breach of a covenant in the lease (most unlikely) or by operation of law is an excluded assignment. The effect of this is that such an assignment will not entitle the landlord (or former landlord) to apply for a release from the lease covenants. However, another right to do so will subsequently arise following the next assignment of the reversion which is not an excluded assignment (s 11(3)).

2.4 POSITION OF INCOMING LANDLORD ON ASSIGNMENT OF THE REVERSION OF A NEW LEASE

As from the date of the assignment, the new landlord becomes bound by the landlord covenants in the lease except to the extent that immediately before the assignment they did not bind the assignor. Similarly, the new landlord becomes entitled to the benefit of the tenant covenants in the lease (s 3(3)). The new landlord can exercise the right of re-entry (but not sue, unless the right to do so has been assigned) in respect of breaches occurring before the assignment (s 23(3)). The new landlord will also acquire the benefit of any existing guarantor covenants: as explained more fully at 8.1.3 the common law rules about covenants which touch and concern the land survive, having only been altered as regards landlord and tenant covenants.

A PRACTITIONER'S VIEW
Tenant release

▷An assignment made in breach of covenant is an excluded assignment and tenant release does not apply (see 2.1). Obviously, the sensible response is that a tenant should always make sure that he obtains his landlord's consent. However, even respectable and responsible tenants may occasionally assign without consent, for example in the case of an assets sale involving many properties, several bidders, little time, or a need for confidentiality. To avoid continuing liability the assignor/selling company could:

- enter into a conditional contract, delaying completion on each property until the landlord's consent has been obtained; or
- grant an immediate underlease to the buyer with an option to acquire the lease once the landlord has given consent. However, this course of action is not appropriate in all cases, as the grant of the underlease itself is likely to be a breach of covenant entitling the landlord to forfeit if consent is not obtained.

▷ At present, leases commonly require an assignee to give a direct covenant to the landlord both to create privity of contract between the landlord and the assignee and to ensure that all the tenant covenants are enforceable. Any such attempt to recreate privity by the back door will be void in new leases (s 25) and will not be necessary to enforce tenant covenants. However, landlords are able to draft new leases with an alienation clause requiring an assignee to offer third party guarantors (in addition to the outgoing tenant under an AGA). Such guarantors will still have to enter into direct covenants but their liability on the guarantee will end when the assignee's liability ends under the Act (s 24(2)). Note that direct covenants extending to the full term may continue to be required in *existing* leases.

▷ There will be no objection to requiring a direct covenant from a sub-tenant provided that liability does not extend beyond the period permitted under the Act. However, there is a trap for the unwary where the lease is an old one but the sub-lease is granted under the new regime. Despite what the lease may say about the sub-tenant covenanting directly with the landlord for the term of the sub-lease, this will be outlawed by section 25 of the Act, and the most that the sub-tenant can be asked to do is to covenant while he is bound by the tenant covenants of the sub-lease. Landlords should consider including in their consent to the sub-letting a condition that successors to the sub-tenant covenant directly with them for the period of their liability under the sub-lease.

Landlord release

▷ In multi-occupied buildings where there are numerous tenants who object to the landlord's notice requesting a release (see 2.3), it is likely that there will be consolidated actions.

▷ However, it seems unlikely that many tenants will object unless they are very sure of their grounds because of the risk of being liable in costs if their objection is not upheld by the courts.

▷ If a landlord is not released on the first disposal, there are further opportunities for release on subsequent disposals of the reversion (see 2.3). In view of this, landlords will want the contract for sale of the reversion to require the purchaser to notify them of the purchaser's own disposal of the property. Without such a provision, an unreleased landlord may not find out in time about the opportunity to apply again for release. See Precedent 5 (page 117) for an example of such a provision.

▷ A landlord who undertakes obligations to construct the property should consider making them personal, so that there can be no question of their binding successors. Conversely, a purchaser of the reversion will want to check the agreement for lease to find out what construction obligations it contained.

▷ Landlords of new leases may (by reason of the 'savings' in section 26) be able to achieve an automatic release upon disposing of the reversion, notwithstanding the Act's general anti-avoidance provisions in section 25. In specific terms, this can be done by making the landlord covenants personal to the original landlord. By virtue of section 3(6)(a) this would prevent them from binding future landlords. The landlord should covenant to obtain similar personal covenants from his immediate successor—see Precedent 7. This will both make the scheme more commercially acceptable to tenants and reduce the possibility that a judge would feel compelled to accept an argument that section 26 is to be read subject to section 25 and that the 'personal' covenants are to be narrowly restricted to covenants which could only be performed by the particular landlord who sought the automatic release. By ensuring that there is always a landlord covenantor, the landlord reduces, but does not eliminate, the possibility of attack.

Excluded assignments

In the past a tenant, being sure that the landlord was unreasonably withholding his consent to assign, could (if the assignee agreed) assign without consent using the landlord's unreasonableness as a defence to any action brought by the landlord for breach of covenant. Tenants should realise that under a new lease such a course of action may not release the tenant from his liability under the lease since, if it turns out that the landlord is acting reasonably, the assignment is an excluded assignment. The best course of action is for the tenant to obtain a declaration from the court as to the landlord's unreasonableness.

authorised guarantee
agreements

3.1 THE CURRENT REGIME

Under the current regime, the fact that the original tenant remains liable on his covenants throughout the term of the lease means that he underwrites the obligations of his assignee. The nature of original tenant liability is such that the position of an original tenant is almost the equivalent of that of a guarantor for all future assignees. However, the difference between an original tenant and a guarantor is that, whilst a guarantor is usually discharged by a variation in the terms of the lease which prejudice the guarantor, the original tenant is not (see 7.1). Furthermore, while if two or more guarantors are liable to the landlord, the release of one will release all of them, the release of an assignee will not release the original tenant (except where there is a release by accord and satisfaction; see *Deanplan Ltd v Mahmoud* [1992] 1 WLR 467).

Under alienation covenants in existing leases, a landlord usually increases the number of persons he can sue in the event of tenant default by including an express requirement in the covenant for any assignee to enter into a direct covenant with the landlord upon assignment. This creates privity of contract between the landlord and assignee in respect of all of the covenants in the lease, and is usually expressed to run for the entire duration of the term. A landlord also usually includes an express requirement that, in the case of a corporate assignee, and if the landlord so requires, the assignee must procure acceptable guarantors to guarantee the obligations of the assignee (which, by virtue of the assignee's direct covenant, run for the entire duration of the term).

Even if not made an express requirement of the alienation covenant, a landlord under an existing lease will often seek to introduce such requirements as a condition of his giving consent to assign. It has always been debatable whether this is permitted by section 19(1)(a) of the 1927 Act.

The Act makes no changes in this area to leases granted before 1 January 1996, or to those exceptional leases granted after that date, but subject to the current regime (see 1.2).

3.2 THE NEW REGIME

The following rules only apply to leases granted on or after 1 January 1996 (but not to those exceptional cases mentioned at 1.2).

For such leases, it has been seen (see 2.1) that section 5 operates to release a tenant from the tenant covenants on assignment, and that, under section 24(2), the tenant's guarantor is released to the same extent.

Requiring the assignee to procure third party guarantors to guarantee the assignee's liabilities to the landlord is still permissible. The requirement can be framed as a condition lawfully imposed under section 19(1)(a) of the 1927 Act on the grant of a licence to assign, or as a condition imposed by a section 19(1A) agreement made pursuant to section 22 of the Act (see chapter 4 below). However, the requirement for direct covenants from assignees on the assignment of a new lease is now prohibited by section 25(1) (see 1.3).

For new leases, an outgoing tenant can be required to guarantee the obligations of his assignee under what is termed an authorised guarantee agreement (an AGA). Section 16(1) states that where, on an assignment, a tenant is to any extent released from a tenant covenant by virtue of the Act, nothing prevents the tenant from entering into an AGA with respect to the performance of that covenant by the assignee.

3.2.1 Qualifying agreements

To qualify as an AGA, the agreement must satisfy the three requirements of section 16(2), which are that:

- it must be an agreement under which the tenant guarantees the performance by the assignee of the covenant (or covenants) from which the tenant has been released;
- it must be entered into in the circumstances set out in section 16(3); and
- its provisions must conform with subsections (4) and (5) of section 16.

The circumstances contained in section 16(3) are straightforward. The AGA can only be entered into if the alienation covenant in the lease is drafted so that an assignment cannot be effected without the consent of the landlord (or some other person, such as a superior landlord), and that consent is given subject to a condition (lawfully imposed) that the tenant enters into an AGA. The alienation covenant could be qualified or absolute, since either imports a requirement to obtain the landlord's consent to an assignment. Whether the condition that the tenant enters into an AGA is lawfully imposed depends upon section 19(1)(a) and the new section 19(1A) of the 1927 Act. Under the new section 19(1A) of the 1927 Act, the landlord can draft the alienation covenant to specify conditions subject to which consent to assignment will be given (see chapter 4). One such condition, lawfully imposed by virtue of the new section 19(1A), may be that an AGA is entered into by every outgoing tenant. Alternatively, if the landlord has not specified conditions for assignment in accordance with section 19(1A), he can fall back upon section 19(1)(a) of the 1927 Act, and lawfully impose a requirement for an AGA as a condition of giving consent to an assignment if, applying the *International Drilling Fluids* criteria (see 4.1.3), it is reasonable to do so.

An AGA must conform with subsections (4) and (5) of section 16. Subsection (4) states that an agreement does not qualify as an AGA to the extent that it purports to impose on the outgoing tenant a requirement to guarantee, in any way, the performance by any person other than the assignee of those covenants from which the tenant has been released. Hence, if the agreement requires the outgoing tenant to guarantee the obligations of his 'assignee and its successors in title', the agreement will fall foul of section 16(4). However, such an agreement would not be rendered null and void. Section 16(4) states that the agreement would not qualify as an AGA *to the extent* that it purports to go too far. Therefore, as a guarantee of the first assignee's obligations, the agreement would be effective. Subsection (4) further states that an agreement will not qualify as an AGA if it imposes on the outgoing tenant any liability, restriction or other requirement in relation to any time after the assignee is himself released from the tenant covenants by the Act.

3.2.2 The terms of the guarantee (s 16(5))

The Act leaves the parties relatively free to specify the terms of the AGA so long as none of its terms frustrate the Act's basic premise of limited duration of liability. Under section 16(5), the guarantee may impose either secondary or primary liability upon the former tenant.

It is envisaged that a typical modern form of commercial guarantee to be found in most general practitioner's precedent books will be adapted for use. Since it is probable that most AGAs will be entered into by reason of a condition imposed by a section 19(1A) agreement, the likely practice of landlords' solicitors will be to append the terms of the AGA to the lease in one of the schedules, in much the same way as landlords presently append surety covenants required of guarantors on assignment.

3.2.3 Effect of disclaimer on the AGA

Section 16(8) provides that the law relating to guarantees (and in particular the rules relating to the release of sureties) are, subject to its terms, applicable in relation to any AGA. Therefore, unless its terms provide to the contrary, an AGA will be discharged by a variation of the terms of the lease which is prejudicial to the former tenant. This may render section 18 (dealing with lease variations, as to which see 7.2) redundant as regards new leases. This is because the liability of former tenants under new leases will be governed by the law relating to the release of guarantors rather than the harsher (but developing) law relating to tenants.

One particular rule of law which is dealt with in section 16 is the rule relating to release of guarantors on disclaimer of the lease. Under sections 178 and 315 Insolvency Act 1986, a tenant's liquidator or trustee in bankruptcy (as the case may be) has the power to disclaim onerous property. The disclaimer releases the current tenant and his guarantor, although it is possible (and common) to impose an obligation on the guarantor to take a fresh lease for the residue of the term in those circumstances. The ability to include such an obligation in an AGA is specifically confirmed by section 16(5)(c).

3.2.4 AGAs with earlier tenants

There are circumstances in which a tenant under a new lease is not released from his covenants on assignment, and so an AGA is not necessary. Assignments by operation of law, or in breach of covenant, are excluded assignments under section 11 (see 2.1.1), and in such cases the outgoing tenant is not released until the next assignment (if any) which is not an excluded assignment. However, at the time of the later release, both the former tenant (or tenants, for there could be a series of excluded assignments) and the assigning tenant will be released from the tenant covenants by the Act. In the usual way, the assigning tenant may be required to enter into an AGA to guarantee the obligations of his assignee. Under section 16(6), the landlord is also able to require the former tenant(s) to enter into an AGA (which is an authorised guarantee agreement for the purposes of section 16) under which he too guarantees the performance of the tenant covenants by the current assignee.

A PRACTITIONER'S VIEW

▷ Landlords should be changing their standard forms of lease now to:

- incorporate an automatic requirement for the assignor to enter into an AGA;
- eliminate any requirements for tenants to give direct covenants; and
- modify the existing forms of guarantee covenant, whether for authorised guarantors or others, so that the guarantor's liability equals in length that of the assignee.

Note that section 24(2) is worded in such a way that a contractual guarantor (i.e. a guarantor other than a former tenant under an AGA) is automatically released when the tenant he is guaranteeing is released from the tenant covenants. Thus the contractual guarantor's guarantee does not, in the absence of specific wording, extend to any period during which the former tenant is an authorised guarantor. It is therefore suggested that, where possible, a future potential guarantor is in fact joined to the lease as a joint tenant not a guarantor, or that the wording of the guarantee embraces the underwriting of the obligation of the tenant both as a tenant and in the capacity of authorised guarantor. The contractual guarantor cannot be compelled to give an AGA himself—the wording of section 16 makes it clear that AGAs are only given by former tenants.

In appropriate circumstances (where section 22 applies—as to which see chapter 4), a landlord might be reasonable in insisting, as a condition of giving consent to assign, that the assignor's liability under an AGA be backed by a further guarantee from the assignor's contractual guarantor. There is, however, a possibility that section 25 might work against such a condition. This is because a condition of this nature might be regarded as frustrating the operation of one of the provisions of the Act. The provision is section 24(2), under which a guarantor is released from his liability when the tenant is released. The release of liability is expressed by section 24(2) to be '. . . to the same extent as the tenant is released from that tenant covenant'. This leaves open the argument that, to the quite separate extent that there is an obligation for the tenant to enter into an AGA and take on the different capacity of guarantor, this is an extent which is not covered by section 24(2); there is therefore no attempt by the condition to create an unlawful extension of the contractual guarantor's liability which, in turn, is caught by section 25.

The judiciary might accept that such a condition was on the right side of the line drawn by section 25. The condition might not be regarded as working against the scheme of the Act because the guarantor would be following the principal liability of the tenant, which is properly continued under the AGA. If, however, it were a condition of the licence to assign that the assignor's guarantor should guarantee the incoming assignee, then this might be seen as going too far, because it would impose a burden upon the guarantor beyond what he originally bargained for, namely a liability linked to the fortunes of the assignee. This burden would be material if, for example, a variation to the lease were agreed which left the assignor with a defence to a claim under section 18, but not the assignee who agreed the variation. Distaste for this extension of liability might lead to a substantive application of section 25 with the effect that the obligation to guarantee performance by the assignee would be unenforceable.

Landlords will be in the safest position if they simply draft the contractual guarantee in the lease at the outset so as to provide cover for the tenant's liability under an AGA. This route is least open to the possibility of successful attack.

▷ Tenants should be aware that, because the AGA can require them to take up a fresh lease in the event of disclaimer of the original lease by the assignee's liquidator or trustee in bankruptcy, the former tenant may have two further periods of liability. First, while the fresh lease is vested in the former tenant; and second, on assignment of that lease, under any AGA he is required to give.

▷ Where an old lease is disclaimed after 1 January 1996 and the landlord is contemplating requiring the guarantor to take up a fresh lease, he should be advised that there is some doubt as to which regime will govern the fresh lease. Logic suggests that, if the guarantee agreement was entered into before 1 January 1996, it will be caught by section 1(3)(a) of the Act and the fresh lease will be subject to the old regime. Where the guarantor is introduced after that date, the lease would on this basis be a new lease. In the latter case, as the terms of the guarantee will not normally allow the landlord to make compensatory changes to the assignment provisions (and the guarantor will have no incentive to agree them), the landlord may prefer to rely on other remedies.

▷ Note that where on an assignment subsequent to an excluded assignment both the current assignor and the former tenant are being released from the tenant covenants, the landlord, under section 16(6), can require the former tenant to enter into an AGA in respect of the current assignee's performance of tenant covenants, but only if he also requires the current assignor to enter into such an agreement. In such a situation, he cannot choose to take an AGA from the former tenant alone.

conditions for assignment

4.1 THE CURRENT REGIME
4.1.1 Protection of the Landlord and Tenant Act 1927

Landlords have always required a certain degree of control over the identity and status of the occupier of premises. While an absolute bar on assignment gives the landlord ultimate control, enabling the landlord to permit or prevent assignments at will, most landlords have, in the past, been content to rely upon a qualified covenant against assigning the whole of the premises. If the alienation covenant is drafted to permit an assignment of the lease, subject to obtaining the landlord's prior written consent, section 19(1)(a) of the 1927 Act provides that, notwithstanding any express provision to the contrary, the landlord's licence or consent is not to be unreasonably withheld.

4.1.2 Protection of the Landlord and Tenant Act 1988 (the 1988 Act)

Section 1 of the 1988 Act strengthens the position of a tenant seeking consent to assign. The 1988 Act applies where the lease contains a fully qualified alienation covenant (whether or not the proviso that the landlord's consent is not to be unreasonably withheld is express or implied by section 19(1)(a) of the 1927 Act). When the tenant has made written application for consent, the landlord owes a duty, within a reasonable time:

- to give consent, unless it is reasonable not to do so. For this purpose, the giving of consent subject to an unreasonable condition breaches the duty; and

- to serve on the tenant written notice of his decision whether or not to give consent, specifying in addition:
    - if the consent is given subject to conditions, the conditions; or
    - if the consent is withheld, the reasons for withholding it.

4.1.3 Reasonableness

Whether the landlord is acting reasonably in withholding consent to assign or in imposing conditions for the assignment has to be judged from the circumstances of each case. The Court of Appeal laid down a number of guidelines on the issue of the landlord's reasonableness in *International Drilling Fluids Ltd v Louisville Investments (Uxbridge) Ltd* [1986] Ch 513.

- The purpose of a fully qualified covenant against assignment is to protect the landlord from having his premises used or occupied in an undesirable way, or by an undesirable tenant or assignee.
- A landlord is not entitled to refuse his consent to an assignment on grounds which have nothing whatever to do with the relationship of landlord and tenant in regard to the subject matter of the lease.
- It is unnecessary for the landlord to prove that the conclusions which led him to refuse to consent were justified, if they were conclusions which might be reached by a reasonable landlord in the circumstances. Although the *International Drilling Fluids* case pre-dated the 1988 Act, the Court of Appeal, in *Air India v Balabel* [1993] 30 EG 90, confirmed that this test was still valid.
- It may be reasonable for the landlord to refuse his consent to an assignment on the ground of the purpose for which the proposed assignee intends to use the premises, even though that purpose is not forbidden by the lease.
- While a landlord need usually only consider his own relevant interests, there may be cases where there is such a disproportion between the benefit to the landlord and the detriment to the tenant if the landlord

withholds his consent to an assignment, that it is unreasonable for the landlord to refuse consent.

• Subject to the above propositions, it is, in each case, a question of fact, depending on all the circumstances, whether the landlord's consent to an assignment is being unreasonably withheld.

Many landlords are of the opinion that the courts have consistently applied the test of reasonableness in the tenant's favour, and have come down heavily upon attempts by landlords to set out in advance what would be a reasonable withholding of consent by the landlord. Under the current regime, the parties to a lease cannot lay down in advance that refusal of consent for a particular reason shall be deemed to be reasonable, since that is a matter for the court to decide. In *Creery v Summersell and Flowerdew & Co* [1949] Ch. 751, a covenant '. . . not to underlet without the consent (not to be unreasonably withheld) of the lessor had and obtained save that the lessor reserves the right not to give his consent if in his opinion the proposed . . . sublessee is for any reason in his discretion undesirable as an occupant . . .' was held to fall foul of section 19(1)(a) of the 1927 Act as it attempted to vest in the landlord rights which went beyond section 19(1)(a) and amounted to an 'express provision to the contrary'. Equally, in *Re Smith's Lease, Smith v Richards* [1951] 1 TLR 254, it was held that a provision that '. . . any refusal by the lessor to consent . . . shall not be deemed to be an unreasonable withholding of consent by reason only that the lessor at the time of intimating any such refusal may offer to accept from the lessee a surrender of the tenancy . . .' was invalid, as the parties could not themselves decide what was, or was not reasonable, and so restrict the operation of section 19(1)(a).

However, a fine line has been drawn between stipulations in the alienation covenant which seek to determine what will or will not be a reasonable withholding of consent, and properly drafted conditions which may be construed as conditions precedent to the operation of the alienation covenant. The Court of Appeal, in *Bocardo S.A. v S & M Hotels* [1980] 1

WLR 17, upheld the validity (under s 19(1)(a)) of a provision which obliged the tenant first to offer to surrender his lease to the landlord before making an application for licence to assign. In *Vaux Group plc v Lilley* [1991] 1 EGLR 60, a case at first instance which related to section 19(1)(b) of the 1927 Act (which is phrased in terms similar to s 19(1)(a)), the court viewed an express provision of the alienation covenant obliging the assignee to procure guarantors to be a valid requirement, quite separate from any restriction on assigning—something which technically was to be performed by the assignee after the assignment had been effected.

Landlords feared that the changes to privity of contract effected by the Act, combined with the existing statutory protection for tenants, and an inability to dictate terms upon which the landlord would be prepared to consent to an assignment, would lead to a dilution of strength of covenant upon assignment. With landlords unable to pursue the party with whom they first chose to do business (i.e. the original tenant), there arose the distinct possibility that landlords in the future would become more inclined to impose absolute bars on assigning, or would impose conditions precedent to be satisfied before the right to assign arose, to retain the requisite degree of control. A compromise was reached in the form of section 22 of the Act.

4.2 THE NEW REGIME

Section 22 introduces new subsections 1(A) to 1(E) into section 19 of the 1927 Act, and allows the landlord and tenant freedom to agree terms upon which the landlord will consent, or circumstances in which he may withhold consent to the tenant's application for licence to assign. While this part of the Act is of considerable comfort to commercial landlords, it was not intended, nor was it thought suitable, to legislate in the residential sector where leases tend to be short and at a rent, or long and at a premium.

Hence, section 22 applies only to a 'qualifying lease', which is defined in section 22 as a lease which is a new tenancy for the purposes of section 1 of the Act (see 1.2), other than a residential lease. A residential lease is one by which a building, or part of a building, is let wholly or mainly as a single private residence. Agricultural tenancies have, of course, always been outside the scope of section 19 of the 1927 Act, and they remain so.

The new additional subsections in section 19 of the 1927 Act relate only to covenants against assigning premises, but by virtue of the new section 19(1E)(b), references to an 'assignment' in the new subsections include a parting with possession on assignment. This is because the standard alienation covenant forbids both assignment and parting with possession of premises without consent, and both elements of the covenant are subject to section 19(1)(a) of the 1927 Act. If the new subsections allowed the landlord lawfully to dictate terms for an assignment, but not a parting with possession, then as the former transaction invariably involves the latter, a situation could theoretically arise whereby the landlord was acting reasonably as regards the assignment, but unreasonably as regards the parting with possession.

4.2.1 Agreeing conditions for assignment

Under the new section 19(1A) of the 1927 Act, if the landlord and tenant have entered into an agreement which specifies circumstances in which the landlord may withhold his consent to an assignment, then the landlord will not be withholding his consent unreasonably if he withholds his consent because any of those circumstances exist. Equally, where such an agreement specifies conditions subject to which consent to an assignment may be granted, the landlord will not be taken to have imposed an unreasonable condition if consent is given subject to one or more of the specified conditions. It should be noted that it is only the landlord under the tenancy who can rely upon the s 19(1A) agreement to provide him with cast-iron reasonable grounds for withholding consent to an assignment. In cases where a superior landlord's consent to the assignment is required, the agreement is of no assistance.

It is provided that section 1 of the 1988 Act shall have effect subject to the new section 19(1A) of the 1927 Act, and clearly, if the parties choose not to agree conditions for assignment in this way, or if the landlord withholds consent on grounds other than those agreed, then the provisions of section 19(1)(a) of the 1927 Act will apply in the usual way.

Considerable scope is therefore given to a landlord to endeavour, through negotiation, to maintain covenant strength, by setting out terms upon which an assignment will be permitted.

The agreement which the parties enter into under section 19(1A) does not necessarily have to be in the lease, although in the vast majority of cases, if such an agreement is to be entered into, it will be found in the alienation covenant. The agreement could, however, be entered into in a side letter to the lease recording an agreement between the landlord, tenant and guarantor (if any), or in a supplemental deed or licence, or indeed in an agreement for lease, but, wherever it is to be found, the new section 19(1B) of the 1927 Act requires that the agreement must be entered into before the tenant's application for licence to assign is made. This prevents a landlord who under the new regime has been remiss in the drafting of the alienation covenant, from introducing as a condition of giving consent to the tenant's application a requirement that the tenant now enters into a section 19(1A) agreement. Such a condition would be subject to section 19(1)(a) of the 1927 Act and would stand or fall upon its reasonableness.

It has been suggested that the words ". . . an agreement specifying for the purposes of this subsection . . ." in the new subsection (1A) to section 19 of the 1927 Act require the draftsman of a new style alienation clause to state that it is entered into pursuant to section 19(1A). It seems unlikely that this is what the statute intends: section 20(2) of the Act is much more explicit when it requires a statement to be included in an overriding lease. A court is likely to regard the words in section 19(1A) as merely explaining the rationale of the agreement. However, cautious landlords will want to mention section 19(1A) specifically to avoid the argument—see Precedent 2, clause D.1.1.

4.2.2 Ineffective agreements

The new section 19(1A) of the 1927 Act does not, however, give the parties complete freedom to impose any terms on assignment. The new section 19(1C) of the 1927 Act restricts the operation of agreements entered into by a landlord and tenant which specify circumstances or conditions requiring a determination of an issue (e.g. whether the assignee is of the requisite financial standing), where that determination is solely within the discretion of the landlord (or some other person). Such a provision will not qualify as an agreement for the purposes of section 19(1A) (and would therefore remain subject to s 19(1)(a)) unless either:

- the discretion vested in the landlord (or other person) is required to be exercised reasonably; or
- the tenant is given an unrestricted right to have the determination reviewed by an independent third party whose identity is ascertainable by reference to the agreement.

4.2.3 Factual or discretionary provisions?

It will be apparent from 4.2.2 above that the circumstances or conditions that the landlord may seek to include in an agreement under section 22 fall into two categories—those which can be factually or objectively verified, and those where the landlord has a discretion.

Factual tests

Typical examples of factual circumstances which the agreement may require to exist before the landlord is obliged to give licence to assign will include a requirement that the proposed assignee must be a publicly quoted company on the London Stock Exchange, or have pre-tax net profits revealed by the assignee's most recently published accounts that equate to the passing rent multiplied by an appropriate multiplier. Factual conditions which the agreement might seek to impose could include requiring the assignee to put up a rent deposit, requiring the assignor to enter into an AGA (see chapter

3), or requiring the assignor to remedy all subsisting breaches of covenant before assigning. Provided they have been clearly drafted, the factual, objective nature of such circumstances or conditions will leave little scope for dispute. The benefit for the tenant will be that he can be sure of what is required in terms of an acceptable assignee. For an example of how to frame a factual test, see Precedent 2, clause D.3.1.

Discretionary tests

Discretionary circumstances or conditions are caught by the new section 19(1C) of the 1927 Act and (see 4.2.2.) will, no doubt, give some scope for dispute, since they must either provide for an independent third party reference, or be the subject of a reasonable (and therefore potentially challengeable) determination by the landlord (or other specified person). Typical examples of discretionary circumstances or conditions may include a provision that the proposed assignee must, in the opinion of the landlord, be of equivalent financial standing to the assignor, and should the tenant not agree, the matter is to be referred to an independent third party; or a provision that the assignee must not, in the reasonable opinion of the landlord, be in competition with the landlord's anchor tenant.

It is not clear from the wording of the new provisions whether, in judging the reasonableness or otherwise of the landlord, existing case law under section 19(1)(a) of the 1927 Act will apply. However, since what is being vested in the landlord is the right to exercise a discretion within the narrow confines of the condition as drafted (as opposed to the wide discretion to grant or withhold consent generally), it is arguable that a court would approach the issue by asking whether this particular landlord, in exercising his discretion, has performed his task in a reasonable way. Nonetheless, a tenant may be able to persuade the court that the issue is whether the landlord has come to a conclusion, in respect of the narrow issue defined by the landlord, that a reasonable landlord would have reached. For an example of how to frame such a test, see Precedent 2, clause D.3.2.

Where the tenant is given a right of appeal to an independent third party, that party's decision must be conclusive, implying that the party is acting as an expert. No criteria for the third party's review of the landlord's decision are set out in the Act, so the parties should spell these out in the lease. For an example of how to frame a test involving a right of appeal, see Precedent 2, clause D.3.3.

4.2.4 Building leases

Alienation covenants contained in building leases have always been subject to slightly different treatment from similar covenants in other leases. A building lease, under section 19(1)(b) of the 1927 Act, is one granted for a term of more than 40 years in consideration wholly or partly of the erection or substantial improvement, addition or alteration of buildings (except where the landlord is a Government department, or local or public authority, or a statutory or public utility company). Under the existing regime, in the case of an assignment or parting with possession of the premises effected more than seven years before the end of the term, any '. . . covenant, condition or agreement against assigning. . .or parting with possession of demised premises or any part thereof without licence or consent . . .' contained in the lease is subject to a proviso that no consent or licence is required if written notice of the transaction is given to the landlord within six months of the transaction being effected. During the last seven years of the term, section 19(1)(a) applies in the usual way. It has always been considered slightly anomalous that such leases should be subject to a different regime as regards provisions restricting alienation.

Under section 22 of the Act, building leases are brought into line with all other leases. Section 22 introduces a new subsection (1D) into section 19 of the 1927 Act which simply provides that as regards a qualifying lease (i.e. a new non-residential lease), section 19(1)(b) of the 1927 Act does not have effect in relation to an assignment of that lease. This leaves the landlord free to attempt to introduce section 19(1A) agreements into new building leases, or allows him to fall back upon section 19(1)(a) of the 1927 Act throughout the duration of the term of the lease.

A PRACTITIONER'S VIEW

▷It is now necessary for landlords' solicitors to re-appraise their standard draft leases to check on the suitability of existing alienation covenants in the light of these changes. Careful drafting will be required of the landlord's solicitor in specifying conditions for assignment, or circumstances which must exist to permit an assignment, since, if the tests the landlord devises are over-stringent or inappropriate, they may be construed as onerous conditions, and may therefore rebound on the landlord at rent review.

▷Different approaches may be considered necessary for different types of properties. For example, in the case of a letting to the anchor tenant of a store in a shopping centre, it may be appropriate to permit assignment of that store only to another national retailer (and careful drafting would be required to define what is meant by a national retailer). For smaller units in the same shopping centre, assignment to a sole trader may be acceptable. Equally, the criteria for offices above a high street shop are likely to be quite different from those for a new landmark office building in the heart of a city's business district. Indeed, in the case of many run of the mill properties, landlords may prefer to leave the lease silent and rely on section 19(1)(a) of the 1927 Act.

▷In the case of institutional lettings, lenders will doubtless want to specify the sort of conditions that the borrower may impose.

▷In cases where the landlord chooses to rely upon discretionary provisions, the need for a possible third party determination will, no doubt, lead to more work for surveyors and accountants.

▷ Landlords should start working now with their agents and solicitors to analyse the precise conditions to frame for each class of asset in the landlord's portfolio. It may be helpful to start with the landlord's current checklist of what is required of an assignee. Some of the items on the list may well be suited to conversion into factual conditions to include in the alienation covenant. A degree of flexibility can be achieved in the drafting by linking the test to the status of the first tenant; for example, if the first named tenant is a public limited company, then any assignee must be such a company too.

▷ Careful thought needs to be given to accepting a tenant who is worthless but backed by a substantial guarantee (e.g. from the parent company or the franchisor). The contractual guarantee ends when the tenant is released from the tenant covenants (i.e. typically on assignment; see s 24(2)). Only the outgoing tenant may be required to give an AGA. Landlords should therefore consider a condition aggregating the covenant strength of the tenant and his guarantor and making that (rather than the financial status of the tenant alone) the standard which assignees have to match, either alone or in combination with their own contractual guarantees, rent deposits or other security.

▷ Conditions comparing the covenant strength of the assignee with that of the assignor should make clear the date at which the assignor's strength is measured. The date of the application for licence to assign may not be appropriate if the reason for the assignment is the assignor's deteriorating financial position.

Furthermore, in devising a test which calls for some form of comparison between assignor and assignee, the landlord should endeavour to achieve an element of certainty to avoid potential dispute. He should consider specifying the factors which are to be taken into account in making the comparison, since it may be the case that, while the assignee matches up to the assignor in some regards, significantly he falls short in others.

▷Landlords should be wary of relying solely upon tests which relate to the assignee's profitability or net worth. The assignee's most recently published accounts might disguise, for instance, the fact that the assignee is currently overstretching itself. A better approach might be to combine such a factual test with a discretionary test relating to the assignee's financial status. Consideration might also be given to devising a factual test based upon the assignee's rating at a recognised credit-rating agency.

▷It should not be overlooked that the new section 19(1A) operates so that if the specified circumstances do not exist, or the conditions have not been met, the landlord is not to be taken to be unreasonably withholding his consent. Where those circumstances do exist, or the conditions have been, or will be met, the landlord may still withhold his consent, but his reasonableness will be determined under the old section 19(1)(a) regime. It remains to be seen whether the fact that the tenant is to obtain a release under the Act will alter the approach of the court to the question of reasonableness.

▷If a prospective assignee does not satisfy the specified conditions, but the landlord is nevertheless willing to consent, the landlord may attach such conditions as he pleases to the consent. Reasonableness (even under s 19(1)(a) of the 1927 Act in its unamended form) is not relevant—although the landlord could not use this as an opportunity to reimpose privity (see s 25(1)).

▷While some landlords will undoubtedly want to set profits and assets tests in factual terms, others will prefer the flexibility of a discretionary condition framed in general terms capable of accommodating the circumstances of the tenant whether an individual, a body corporate or a public authority. For example, the landlord might provide that the tenant must ensure that the assignee is a person who in the reasonable opinion of the landlord is plainly capable of observing the covenants of the lease and who is likely to remain so in the future.

▷Some landlords will want to introduce a test to the effect that the tenant must, before assigning, establish to the landlord's reasonable satisfaction that all payments have been made up to date and that other covenants have been materially performed. The word "materially" is important. A requirement of absolute performance could make the lease impossible to assign. The Act appears to require those drafting alienation clauses to take care to distinguish between 'circumstances' and 'conditions'. This point is dealt with in more detail in a note to Precedent 2.

tenant default: **liability of former tenant (or his guarantor) for 'fixed charges'**

The following provisions apply to all leases, whenever granted.

Under the law as it stands before 1 January 1996, the first a former tenant or his guarantor may learn of problems encountered by the current tenant is when the landlord sends to him a large demand, perhaps for several years' back rent. Former tenants were aggrieved at their continuing liability in the first place and an 'out of the blue' demand for payments covering long periods of arrears only made matters worse. The Act aims to give former tenants and their guarantors who find themselves in that unfortunate position prior notice of potential claims against them.

The prior notice is referred to as a 'default notice' in this book.

The default notice provisions only apply to what the Act calls a 'fixed charge'.

5.1 WHAT IS A 'FIXED CHARGE'?

Section 17 of the Act defines a 'fixed charge' to mean:

* rent;
* service charge, as defined in section 18 of the Landlord and Tenant Act 1985 (and thus including insurance charges);
* any liquidated sum payable under the lease for failure to comply with a tenant covenant.

    For example, a provision in the lease requiring the tenant to pay £1,000 for every day that the tenant is in breach of a keep open covenant. Such a provision is currently uncommon but might recommend itself to an anxious and far-sighted tenant who is keen to cap the damages payable by an assignee (thus preventing a landlord arguing for greater damages in respect of damage to an enlarged reversionary interest) and to obtain a default notice in respect of those damages.

Unless a sum falls within the definition of a fixed charge there is no requirement for the landlord to serve a default notice. The definition does not appear to extend to damages which only become quantified after a court order is obtained. If this is right, then, for example, if the landlord obtains damages against the current tenant for breach of the user clause, no default notice need be served on any former tenant or guarantor who may be equally liable with the current tenant. This interpretation of the wording is supported by the debate reported in *Hansard* (Volume 263 No. 138 at page 1256). However, if a covenant specifically requires the tenant to pay 'a liquidated sum set out in a court order' then it is just possible on the wording used by the section that a court would hold that any sum thus set out would qualify as a fixed charge, although such a result is unlikely.

5.2 THE DEFAULT NOTICE

The basic rule is that a landlord who wishes to pursue a former tenant or his guarantor for a fixed charge, must serve on that person, within six months of the current tenant's default, a default notice setting out details of the potential claim. Failure to do so means that the landlord will be unable to recover that sum from the person(s) concerned.

5.2.1 Who must be served with a default notice?

The list of former tenants and guarantors against whom a landlord may wish to pursue a claim for a fixed charge (and upon whom, therefore, a default notice may be served) is:

for leases granted before 1 January 1996 (and the exceptional cases at 1.2):

• the original tenant, who may remain liable by virtue of privity of contract; or

- previous tenants who have given the landlord a direct covenant on assignment, upon which they remain liable; or
- guarantors of former tenants;

for new leases:

- a former tenant who remains liable under his AGA; or
- a former tenant who has not been released because the assignment was an excluded assignment (see 2.1.2); or
- a guarantor of either of the above who has not been released.

Note that neither regime requires a default notice to be given to the contractual guarantor of the current tenant.

5.2.2 Content of a default notice

There is a prescribed form of default notice. It must inform the recipient:

- that the fixed charge is now due; and
- that the landlord intends to recover from the recipient the amount specified in the notice and (where payable) interest at a specified rate.

Section 17(4) caters for the situation where the exact amount of the fixed charge is still subject to determination and might therefore increase at some stage after service of the default notice (e.g. a rent subject to review). The increase will only be recoverable by the landlord if the default notice informs the recipient of the possibility of an increased liability, and a further notice is served within three months of the determination of that increase.

5.2.3 When must the default notice be served?

The default notice must be served within six months from the date when the fixed charge became due.

Any fixed charge which has become due before 1 January 1996 is treated as becoming due on 1 January 1996 and thus landlords will have six months from then to serve default notices in respect of fixed charges which fell due before that date. If proceedings have already been instituted against the former tenant before 1 January 1996, no default notice needs to be served on the former tenant or his guarantor (presumably on the basis that the notice would not tell him anything he did not already know). However, if the landlord had instituted proceedings against the guarantor alone, a default notice would still need to be served on the guarantor (see s 17(5)).

5.2.4 Effect of failure to serve a default notice

Unless a valid default notice for the fixed charge is served in time, the former tenant and his guarantor will cease to be liable for it. Take, for example, a case where the current tenant does not pay the rent due on 25 March, 24 June and 29 September. The landlord could serve three default notices in, say, April, July and October, each relating to one quarter's rent. Alternatively, the landlord could serve the first notice in July relating to both the March and the June rent. However, the Act operates on months, not quarters, and if the landlord has not served a default notice by 25 September in relation to the March quarter's rent, that rent will not be recoverable from the former tenant, although the landlord would still be in time to serve notice to preserve the right to recover the June rent.

5.2.5 What can the recipient do following payment?

A former tenant or his guarantor who makes full payment under a default notice may be able to regain some control over the property and discipline the current (and defaulting) tenant by calling for an overriding lease from the landlord (see chapter 6).

A PRACTITIONER'S VIEW

▷Landlords may be concerned about the difficulties of tracing former tenants in time to serve a default notice to preserve their rights. In the case of companies, service can, of course, be effected at the registered office, which is readily ascertainable. In the case of individuals, service can be at their last known place of abode (s 27(5) of the Act and s 23 of the 1927 Act). Ultimately, if the whereabouts of a former tenant cannot be easily ascertained, the landlord will have to decide how much time and effort he is prepared to spend on pursuing a former tenant who may not be able to pay in any event.

▷ Landlords may also want to consider carefully whether to serve default notices on all former tenants and guarantors, as payment under a default notice entitles the payer to call for an overriding lease (see chapter 6). Where the sums involved are large or the landlord has reason to believe a weak former tenant is anxious to regain possession, the landlord may prefer to serve just one default notice on the person he perceives to be the most financially sound. If the landlord serves a default notice on a financially weaker person and that person takes up an overriding lease and then forfeits the occupational lease, the landlord will be left with remedies only against that weaker person. Forfeiture of the occupational lease results in the loss of all the collateral covenants underpinning the covenants of the occupational tenant (e.g. the covenants of guarantors, including those under AGAs, and of those who, pursuant to existing leases, were original tenants or directly covenanting assignees).

▷ In negotiating leases (whether before or after the Act comes into force), tenants may wish to extend the circumstances in which a default notice needs to be served (e.g. to all cases of breach of covenant irrespective of whether the damages are set out in the lease or ascertained after the breach is committed—see Precedent 3).

the overriding lease

The following provisions apply to all leases, whenever granted.

Under the law as it stands before 1 January 1996, a former tenant (or his guarantor) may be in the unenviable position of being liable for the current tenant's default, but with no power over him nor any right to regain control of the premises (subject to his ability to obtain a vesting order under the Insolvency Act 1986 following disclaimer of the lease). The mechanism of the overriding lease is designed to deal with both of these shortcomings. If a former tenant, or guarantor, makes full payment under a default notice, the Act allows him to claim an overriding lease from the landlord within 12 months. The effect of an overriding lease is that the claimant becomes the defaulting tenant's immediate landlord.

For example, L grants a lease to T before 1 January 1996. This lease is now owned by A who falls into arrears with his rent. L serves a default notice on T requiring T to pay the rent (under the old privity regime). T makes payment in full and claims an overriding lease from L. This will be a headlease 'slotted in' above the lease held by A (the defaulting tenant). A's occupational lease simply moves one step down the reversionary line and becomes a sub-lease. The tenant under the overriding lease enjoys the benefit of the tenant covenants in the occupational lease and has the benefit of the right of re-entry in that lease. The overriding lease thus gives T some control over the premises for which he is being held liable including the right to forfeit the occupational lease (sub-lease) for breach of covenant.

A similar situation arises in respect of leases granted on or after 1 January

1996 where a former tenant has been required under an AGA to guarantee the performance of his immediate assignee. If the assignee falls behind with the rent, the service by the landlord of a default notice on the former tenant may trigger a claim by him for an overriding lease.

6.1 WHO CAN CLAIM AN OVERRIDING LEASE?

The right to call for an overriding lease is only conferred on the recipient of a default notice who makes full payment of the specified fixed charge (together with any interest payable).

It is possible (but perhaps not very likely) that more than one person will be served with a default notice, make payment in full, and call for an overriding lease. Consider the position where the tenant has been in arrears for twelve months or more. The landlord may have served a series of default notices and different former tenants may have paid in full the June and September quarter respectively. In October both former tenants may claim an overriding lease. In such a situation the overriding lease will be granted to the person who makes his request first (see below). If two or more requests for an overriding lease are made on the same day, section 19(8) provides that a request made by a person who was liable as a former tenant has priority over a request made by someone who was liable as a guarantor; and, subject to that, earlier covenantors have priority over later ones.

It is also possible that at some time after a proper request has been made for an overriding lease, the occupational tenant will tender a rental payment. However, this payment cannot be accepted in respect of the rental period for which the former tenant or guarantor has already paid. The right to the overriding lease will not be cancelled by the current tenant's attempt to make the payment.

6.2 HOW MANY OVERRIDING LEASES CAN THERE BE?

Where a lease has been assigned several times, more than one overriding lease may arise. For example, L grants a lease to T before 1 January 1996.

It is assigned to A1, then A2 and finally to A3. A3 defaults on the rent. L serves a default notice on T who pays in full and takes an overriding lease from L. The chain of title is now L→T→A3. A3 continues to default. T, having acquired the benefit of the direct covenants given by A1 and A2 to T, decides not to forfeit. T serves a default notice on A1 who pays in full and takes an overriding lease from T. The chain of title is now L→T→A1→A3. If, on the other hand, T forfeits A3's lease, the covenants of A1 and A2 (and their guarantors) would be released. If T later defaults under his overriding lease, L has no recourse against anyone else. Commercially, however, the risk is remote because a landlord will consider carefully which of his former tenants to serve with a default notice in the first place, in the knowledge that the notice may trigger a claim for an overriding lease. The landlord should avoid pursuing any former tenant who is weak or otherwise undesirable unless absolutely necessary.

If the above example had involved a new lease, only A2 (under his AGA) would be liable to L for the default of A3, and thus it would be A2 calling for an overriding lease following payment under L's default notice.

6.3 HOW IS AN OVERRIDING LEASE CLAIMED?

The claimant must make his request to the landlord in writing specifying the payment which entitles him to an overriding lease. There is no prescribed form. The request must be made at the time the claimant makes payment or within 12 months of that date (s 19(5)). Any such request should be protected by a notice or caution under the Land Registration Act 1925 (or, in the case of unregistered reversions, by registration of an estate contract under the Land Charges Act 1972). Following receipt of a valid request the landlord must grant the claimant an overriding lease within a reasonable time (s 19(6)). If the landlord does not, the claimant may bring an action in tort for breach of statutory duty (s 20(3)). The claimant is responsible for the landlord's reasonable costs in connection with the grant of the overriding lease and must, following grant of the overriding lease, deliver a counterpart of it to the landlord.

Until the claimant has delivered a counterpart of the lease, he will be unable to exercise any rights under the overriding lease (s 20(3)).

6.4 WHAT ARE THE TERMS AND CONTENT OF THE OVERRIDING LEASE?

As a general rule, the overriding lease will be granted on terms identical to the defaulting tenant's lease (unless the claimant and the landlord agree otherwise). However, it will not be possible simply to duplicate the covenants in the overridden lease. Certain adjustments will be necessary to:

- add a small reversionary period, usually three days (s 19(2));
- omit from the overriding lease any personal or spent covenants in the defaulting tenant's lease (ss 19(3) and (4));
- ensure that where, under the defaulting tenant's lease, any right, liability or other matter falls to be determined by reference to the commencement of that tenancy, the corresponding provision of the overriding lease also operates by reference to that date (s 19(4)). This will be important as far as repair covenants, break clauses and rent review provisions are concerned.

A former tenant contemplating taking up an overriding lease should scrutinise carefully the disregard of tenant's improvements in the defaulting tenant's lease. This may need modification to avoid improvements made by the defaulting tenant being taken into account on a rent review under the overriding lease. Section 19(2)(b) requires the overriding lease to contain ". . . the same covenants as the relevant tenancy, as they have effect immediately before the grant of the [overriding] lease." The definition of covenants under the Act includes terms, conditions and obligations, and is therefore wide enough to embrace a rent review clause. Unless there is an appropriate modification of the rent review clause (ensuring that both tenant's and sub-tenant's improvements are disregarded), using the same words as in the original lease may not produce the same effect, as required by the Act.

In most cases the problem will not actually arise, as the rent review disregard will specifically cover improvements by sub-tenants (as the defaulting tenant has become) or, if restricted to tenant's improvements, the definition of tenant will include those deriving title from the tenant. In the residue of cases, the Act does allow a suitable modification, although it does not go out of its way to alert the parties to the problem.

Where the landlord's interest is mortgaged, the grant of an overriding lease is deemed to be authorised by the mortgagee (s 20(4)). There is no equivalent provision where the landlord is himself a tenant under a lease requiring consent to underlet. While it is considered that the statutory duty to grant the overriding lease should be a sufficient defence, the cautious landlord may consider it appropriate to obtain formal consent from the superior landlord.

Each overriding lease must contain a statement (see s 20(2)):

- that it is granted pursuant to section 19 of the Act; and
- whether or not it is a new lease for the purposes of the Act. This is important because whether it is an existing or new lease will determine which privity regime applies. Section 20(1) provides that an overriding lease shall only be a new lease if the lease it overrides is a new lease (and thus it follows the privity regime in that lease).

The Land Registry will formulate rules for such statements.

A PRACTITIONER'S VIEW

▷Before deciding to call for an overriding lease a former tenant (or guarantor) should be made aware that:

- he will become liable for the landlord's covenants in the occupational lease, some of which may be onerous;
- he will lose his protection from those variations which have taken place since he assigned the lease but which were not binding upon him as a former tenant (see chapter 7);

- on assignment of the overriding lease he may, if it is a new lease, be required to enter into an AGA;
- stamp duty will be payable on the grant of the overriding lease.

▷ The right to the overriding lease is linked to the service of a default notice (see above). No person can call for an overriding lease unless they have received a default notice. This leaves a small gap in protection for existing leases. For example, consider the position where, following default by the current tenant, the landlord serves a default notice on the original tenant who pays up in full and the original tenant then claims on an indemnity given to him by an intermediate assignee. The intermediate assignee must pay up but has no right to claim an overriding lease since the demand came from the original tenant and not in the form of a default notice from the landlord.

Consider therefore in leases granted under the current regime an amendment to the effect that, if the lease is assigned, the assignee will have a right upon indemnifying the assignor to call upon the landlord to grant the assignee an overriding lease as if the Act applied and the landlord had served a default notice on and been paid by the assignee (not the assignor). (Such a provision will not be required under the new regime where former tenants are only liable by virtue of AGAs.) Alternatively, if it is too late to amend the lease, the assignee can make appropriate provision in the contract for assignment to him. The contract can be drafted to give the assignee the right to require the assignor to call for an overriding lease in a situation where the assignor pays up under a default notice and then makes a claim on the assignee under the indemnity. The assignee should then have the right to take an assignment of the overriding lease or, if that is not permitted by the landlord, be granted an underlease between the overriding lease and the occupational lease. See Precedent 4.

▷One of the benefits of an overriding lease is the right it provides for the claimant to forfeit the occupational lease for breach of covenant. However, this right may not be available in respect of the arrears of rent which triggered the call for the overriding lease in the first place. As noted above, an overriding lease can only be claimed upon making full payment of the fixed charge referred to in the landlord's default notice. It is arguable that the landlord's acceptance of this sum amounts to a waiver of the right to forfeit (being an unequivocal act recognising the continued existence of the lease). This is particularly so where the rent is payable in advance. That being the case, the right to forfeit the occupational lease for those arrears has already been lost before the overriding lease is granted.

Furthermore, even though the former tenant or guarantor acquiring an overriding lease enjoys the benefit of the tenant covenants in the occupational lease, he will not have a right in his new capacity as landlord to pursue the occupational tenant for the arrears of rent referred to in the landlord's default notice since that rent must have been paid as a precondition to calling for an overriding lease. Thus there are no arrears outstanding under the occupational lease. However, where the person out of pocket was the assignor of the occupational lease to the assignee, then, if good conveyancing practice is adopted, the assignment will contain an obligation for the assignee to keep the assignor indemnified. Where indemnity rights are absent, then it is probable that a subrogation claim will be available.

▷Section 19(2)(a) of the Act requires an overriding lease to be granted ". . . for a term equal to the remainder of the term of the relevant tenancy plus three days." This may cause problems where the contractual term has ended but section 24 of the 1954 Act operates to continue the tenancy. It would seem that the term of any overriding lease granted at that time could not exceed three days. Consider, then, the position where the defaulting tenant has vacated the premises without having served notice under section 27 of the 1954 Act, and the landlord serves a default notice for unpaid rent on the former tenant. The tenancy (and the former tenant's liability) will continue indefinitely under the 1954 Act unless the former tenant can engineer a method to bring it to an end. The problem for the former tenant is that if he calls for an overriding lease the term of it may not exceed three days, and within that space of time, it is unlikely that the overriding tenant would have cause to re-enter the premises to end the occupational lease. In such circumstances, the former tenant might be better advised to follow a more traditional route (if available). For example, if the occupational tenant is insolvent the former tenant could consider applying for a vesting order in respect of the tenancy following the liquidation of the occupational tenant and disclaimer by the liquidator. Notice could then be served under section 27 of the 1954 Act.

▷A former tenant may have a contractual right to an overriding lease contained in a lease completed before the commencement of the Act. Such a right is unaffected by the Act and the former tenant will have a choice between the statutory and contractual rights.

chapter 7

lease variations

7.1 THE CURRENT REGIME
7.1.1 Effect on tenants

In the past, one of the most unjust aspects of original tenant liability was that, following an assignment, an original tenant (and the direct covenantees) remained bound by all of the covenants in the lease, including those which had been varied in a manner which increased the tenant's potential liability despite the absence of knowledge or consent.

A tenant may, for example, have entered into a lease on the basis of a narrow user covenant. Following assignment of that lease, the landlord and assignee may agree to vary the lease to permit uses which, while more beneficial to the assignee, are potentially more lucrative to the landlord at rent review. At the next rent review, the rent may well be increased to reflect, in part, the wider permitted use. Should the assignee subsequently stop paying the rent, the original tenant has been held liable for the full amount of the rent, even though in his original bargain with the landlord, a narrower user covenant had been contemplated for the entire duration of the term. This concept is not one to which original tenants have been easily reconciled, and, not surprisingly, attempts have been made over the years to release the original tenant from his liability in such circumstances, either wholly, or at least to the extent that the variation has increased his liability.

In *GUS Property Management Ltd v Texas Homecare Ltd* [1993] 27 EG 130, the original tenant argued that he was only bound to pay a rent which was fixed between landlord and assignee in accordance with the rent review clause in the lease, and that where the assignee had agreed to pay a stepped rent (£210,000 per annum for the first three years of the review period, and £220,000 for the remaining two years) which was not contemplated by the review clause, his liability was either restricted to the amount of rent which would have been payable but for the agreement between landlord and assignee, or completely discharged by variation. While appreciating the force of the original tenant's arguments as a matter of contract law, the court felt unable to depart from the Court of Appeal decision in *Baynton v Morgan* (1888) 22 QB 74, where Lord Esher MR stated that when the original tenant assigns his lease, he '. . . gives to his assignee the powers which he might himself have exercised.' Hence, in *Baynton*, the original tenant remained bound by his covenants notwithstanding that the assignee had varied the lease by surrendering part of the demised premises.

However, in *Friends' Provident Life Office v British Railways Board* [1995] EGCS 140, the Court of Appeal had an opportunity to review the principles of tenant liability in relation to lease variations, and whilst expressing an opinion that the decisions in several earlier cases (*Centrovincial Estates plc v Bulk Storage Ltd* [1983] P & CR 41, *Selous Street Properties Ltd v. Oronel Fabrics Ltd* [1984] 1 EGLR 50 and *GUS Property Management Ltd v Texas Homecare Ltd* above) were ultimately correct, the court held that they were reached upon a misinterpretation of the decision in *Baynton v Morgan*. Sir Christopher Slade said: "The assignment of a lease does not destroy the privity of contract which exists between the landlord and the original tenant; in the result, the original tenant remains liable on all his covenants contained in the original lease, notwithstanding the assignment. If the contract embodied in the original lease itself provides for some variation in the future of the obligations to be performed by the tenant (for example by a rent review clause), the original tenant may be bound to perform the obligations as so varied, even though the variations occur after the assignment of the lease—this will depend on the construction of the relevant covenant(s) in the original lease. If, on the other hand, an assignee of the lease, by arrangement with the landlord agrees to undertake some obligation not contemplated by the contract contained in the original lease, the estate may be altered, but the variation does not affect the obligations of the original tenant."

The propositions made by the Court of Appeal pre-empt, to a large extent, the changes introduced by section 18 of the Act (see below). However, it remains to be seen whether the *Friends' Provident* case can come to the aid of a former tenant whose liability is increased following a rent review which takes into account variations agreed between landlord and assignee. Many rent review clauses provide for the rent to be revised by reference to a hypothetical letting of the premises on the terms of the tenant's actual letting "as varied from time to time". Arguably, therefore, an original tenant's contract may contemplate an increase in liability by reference to subsequent variations. However the better view may be that there is a distinction between, on the one hand, the parties contemplating in the original contract that the rent may increase, and setting out a mechanism for determining it (with safeguards for the tenant in the form of disregards) and, on the other hand, a variation of an unspecified provision of the lease, which may or may not take place, and for which no supporting machinery is provided. A former tenant might hope that a court would grasp at this distinction and relieve him from increased liability.

7.1.2 Effect on guarantors

The position of a guarantor has always been clearly stated. Any variation in the terms of the lease which would prejudice the guarantor will discharge the guarantor unless he has consented to the change (see *Holme v Brunskill* (1878) 3 QBD 495). Accordingly, landlords have frequently drafted surety covenants so that they are stated to apply '. . . notwithstanding that the terms of this lease have been varied by the parties.'

7.1.3 Surrender and regrant

On occasions, the variation of a lease may be so substantial as to effect an implied surrender and regrant at common law, which would have the effect of releasing the original tenant. Whether a variation of the lease amounts to a surrender and regrant depends on the nature of the variation. If additional land is added to the tenancy for an increase in rent, or if the landlord and tenant agree to extend the duration of the term, the effect will be an implied surrender of the existing lease and the grant of a new lease.

The basic test is whether the variation can be effected without the grant of a new lease. In *Friends' Provident Life Office v British Railways Board* (above), the Court of Appeal held that in a case where, following a variation, there was neither an increase in the extent of premises demised by the lease nor an increase in the length of term, there was no reason why the variation should take effect as an implied surrender and regrant for the remainder of the term.

7.2 THE NEW REGIME

7.2.1 The tenant's liability

As mentioned above, section 18 has, to a large extent, been pre-empted by the decision in *Friends' Provident*. However, the aim of the new regime is to provide statutory rules to ensure that no former tenant, or his guarantor, has his liability under the lease increased by reason of changes to the terms of the lease which the landlord had no obligation to allow when the tenant parted with his interest. Under section 18, the liability of former tenants (and their guarantors) to pay to the landlord any sum which is attributable to variations of the lease taking place after the former tenant has assigned is restricted.

1. Which leases are affected?

Section 18 applies to all leases, whenever granted.

Existing leases

In relation to existing leases, section 18 does not apply to any lease variation effected before 1 January 1996 (see s 18(6)). In such a case, the tenant must rely upon *Friends' Provident.* If a former tenant suffers an increase in his liability as a result of a variation effected on or after 1 January 1996, he can seek the protection of section 18.

New leases

Initially, it might be thought that section 18 has little relevance to new leases, because, of course, under a new lease, a tenant is released from liability under the tenant covenants on assignment (see 2.1, and s 5), and therefore should not be too concerned that the lease is subsequently varied. However, a former tenant may still remain liable on the tenant covenants under a new lease by virtue of an AGA under section 16 of the Act (see 3.2), and so the provisions of section 18 are relevant to leases granted under the new regime.

2. Which variations are caught?

Section 18 only applies to 'relevant variations' which are defined by section 18(4) as being ones which are made at a time when:

- the landlord has an absolute right to refuse to allow the variation; or
- if the landlord does not at that time have such a right (because, for instance, the landlord and assignee had agreed to vary the lease to take away the landlord's absolute right), he would have had such a right had the request to vary the lease been made immediately before the former tenant assigned the lease.

In considering whether the landlord has an absolute right to refuse to allow a variation at any particular time, regard must be had to any relevant statutory provisions (see s 18(5)). So, for example, a tenant may be subject to an absolute covenant against making certain alterations to the premises, but under section 3 of the 1927 Act, provided the tenant's alterations are qualifying improvements for the purposes of section 3, and the tenant follows the correct procedure for authorisation of his improvements, the tenant is able to effect his improvements even in the face of an absolute covenant. Hence, in such circumstances, the landlord does not have an absolute right to refuse to allow the alteration, and the former tenant will be liable for any increase in rent attributable to it.

As regards user covenants, an absolute covenant gives the landlord an unfettered right to refuse to allow a change. If a change is allowed, it represents a variation of the lease. One form of qualified covenant against changing the use of premises (e.g. 'not to change the use without the landlord's consent') gives the landlord the same unfettered right to refuse consent to a change of use as does an absolute user covenant (there being no statutorily implied proviso that the landlord's consent is not to be unreasonably withheld). It might be argued that granting consent to a change of use pursuant to that type of covenant is not a variation of the lease, because consent in such a case merely operates as permission within the operation of a covenant which continues to remain in full force and effect. If this argument is accepted, the former tenant would be bound by the consequences of consent. However, it is considered unlikely that the courts will accept this view, depending as it does on a very narrow construction of the word 'variation'.

A fully qualified covenant (e.g. 'not to change the use without the landlord's consent, such consent not to be unreasonably withheld') would doubtless impose post-assignment liability in respect of consents which the landlord, acting reasonably, was bound to give. However, it might be argued by a former tenant that, although the landlord gave consent under the covenant, the landlord nevertheless had reasonable grounds for withholding consent, and was therefore possessed, in the circumstances, of an absolute right to refuse to allow the variation.

Variations can come in many different forms, for example, formal deeds of variation; licences to assign, to alter or to change use; side letters; rent review memoranda. Section 18(7) provides that a variation within the meaning of section 18 means a variation whether effected by deed or otherwise.

3. How does section 18 work?

Section 18 operates first, in the case of new leases, where a former tenant has, under an AGA, guaranteed the performance by his assignee of any tenant covenant in the lease and second, in the case of other leases, where a former tenant remains bound by a tenant covenant, either as original tenant, or by virtue of a direct covenant given to the landlord on assignment.

Where a former tenant remains liable in either of those ways, he will not be liable to pay any amount to the landlord in respect of a tenant covenant, to the extent that it is referable to a relevant variation of the lease effected after the former tenant assigned the lease.

Some examples of how section 18 and the decision in *Friends' Provident* work may assist.

Example 1

Under a lease granted in 1992 at a rent of £10,000 per annum, T's use of the premises is restricted absolutely to a newsagent's shop. In 1994, following an assignment, L and A agree to vary the user covenant to permit the sale of videos, in return for an increase in rent of £500 per annum. In 1996, L and A agree to vary the user covenant further to permit the sale of wine, beer and spirits, in return for a further increase in rent of £1,000 per annum. On default in payment of rent by A, T is not liable for the initial £500 increase, since, although his increased liability in that regard is referable to a variation effected before 1 January 1996, the decision in *Friends' Provident* will come to his aid. As regards the second increase, this results from a relevant variation effected on or after 1 January 1996, which has had the effect of increasing the liability of the former tenant, and so section 18 applies. T cannot therefore be required to pay any part of the second increase, and his maximum liability for rent as original tenant is £10,000 per annum (subject to review).

Example 2

Under a lease granted in 1996 at a rent of £20,000 per annum, subletting of part of the premises is absolutely prohibited. In 1998, to enable T to assign, L grants licence to assign, and agrees in the licence to assign to vary the lease to allow subletting of permitted parts of the premises. T assigns to A, and is released from the tenant covenants under section 5, but enters into an AGA under section 16. At the first rent review in 2001, the rent is increased to £22,000 per annum, reflecting in part the more flexible covenant against subletting part. On default in payment of rent by A, T cannot invoke section 18 to restrict his liability under the AGA. Even though the increased rent partly reflects a relevant variation, the variation was effected in the licence to assign, before T assigned the lease, and so section 18 does not apply. For the same reason, the decision in *Friends' Provident* will not assist T.

7.2.3 The guarantor's liability

The position of guarantors was dealt with at 7.1.2, and often a variation of the lease will operate to discharge the guarantor. Should the guarantor not be discharged at common law by the variation, or should the landlord have the benefit of a clause in the surety covenants purporting to maintain the guarantor's liability notwithstanding any variation of the lease, section 18(4) will apply. Here, it is provided that where a guarantor has agreed to guarantee the performance of a tenant covenant by a former tenant, the guarantor is not liable to pay any sum under the guarantee to the extent that it is referable to a relevant variation. The use of the words 'former tenant' must be appreciated here. Section 18(4) only operates to limit a guarantor's liability in respect of a guarantee of the obligations of someone who is no longer the tenant. If there is a variation of the lease during the tenure of the tenant whose obligations are guaranteed, resulting in an increase in liability under the guarantee, the protection of section 18(4) does not apply. (The general law of guarantees may, however, assist; see for example *West Horndon Industrial Park Ltd. v Phoenix Timber Group plc* [1995] 20 EG 137.)

7.2.4 Dangers of an implied surrender and regrant

Should the variation be so substantial as to effect an implied surrender and regrant of the lease (see 7.1.3), liability under the surrendered lease (as original tenant, guarantor, assignee under a direct covenant, or assignor under an AGA) will end, and the new lease impliedly granted will take effect under the new privity regime.

A PRACTITIONER'S VIEW

▷When the rent has been increased following a variation of the lease (whether as the immediate price of the variation, or on subsequent review), and the landlord wishes to serve a default notice on a former tenant or guarantor (see chapter 5), the landlord will have to calculate what the rental liability of the tenant would have been without the variation. However, the landlord may prefer to specify in the notice the full amount of rent due from the current tenant, to avoid the possibility that any apportionment is not upheld.

▷A former tenant or guarantor who receives a default notice, or receives a demand in the case of sums not covered by the default notice procedure, should always enquire whether the lease has been varied since his disposal of it.

▷Where landlords have an absolute discretion to withhold consent to a variation, they should remember that certain changes (e.g. extending the length of the lease) are so fundamental that they operate as a surrender of the old lease and the grant of a new one. Even under the present law, this releases former tenants and guarantors absolutely and, once the Act is in force, it would give the current tenant the benefit of the new privity regime.

If such a variation is to be permitted, the landlord will want to introduce appropriate conditions for assignment as part of the price for consent.

▷ In its application to new leases, it is interesting to note that a former tenant is only protected by section 18 where he has entered into an AGA with the landlord in respect of his immediate assignee. In certain circumstances, a former tenant can be required to enter into an AGA in respect of a subsequent assignee. In such a case, section 18 does not apply but the former tenant can rely upon the decision in *Friends' Provident* in respect of variations occurring after he has assigned. An example of how this could happen is where the (former) tenant assigns in breach of covenant. This is an excluded assignment (see s 11), and so the (former) tenant does not get his release under section 5, and does not therefore enter into an AGA. On the next assignment which is not an excluded assignment, the (former) tenant is released under section 11(2), but may be required, under s 16(6), to enter into an AGA in respect of the performance of the tenant covenants by the assignee under that subsequent assignment. The protection under section 18 for former tenants under new leases only applies where the former tenant has guaranteed the obligations of his own assignee, and not subsequent assignees, and therefore in this situation the protection would be lost. Curiously, the former tenant would be protected by section 18 during the period between making the excluded assignment and the assignment which ultimately releases him, by virtue of section 18(1)(b).

▷ Only former tenants and their guarantors are protected by section 18. Former landlords who remain unreleased may have further obligations placed upon them when a subsequent landlord agrees with the tenant, say, to give more extensive service obligations following a refurbishment. However, the decision in *Friends' Provident* is wide enough to embrace landlords' contractual obligations, as well as tenants'.

▷Landlords should take note of the possibility of arguing that there is no variation of the lease (and therefore former tenants remain liable) in a case where a landlord sets out in any covenant of the lease a series of possible consents subject always to the tenant obtaining the landlord's permission, which could be arbitrarily refused (e.g. 'to use as a baker's shop or, with the landlord's consent, as a betting shop'). Tenants should beware of this drafting technique which offers them nothing and leaves them having to argue that any such change after the assignment is a variation resulting in the protection of section 18.

chapter 8

miscellaneous points

8.1 TRANSMISSION OF THE BENEFIT AND BURDEN OF COVENANTS

8.1.1 The current regime

The existing law relating to the running of the benefit and burden of covenants in leases is a mixture of statutory provision and long-standing common law rules.

The landlord's reversion

Transmission on the assignment of the landlord's reversion is dealt with by sections 141 and 142 of the Law of Property Act 1925 (LPA 1925). Section 141(1) provides that, on an assignment of the reversion, the rent reserved by the lease and the benefit of every covenant contained in it and having reference to the subject matter of the lease, will run with the reversionary estate. Section 142(1) deals with the burden of the landlord's covenants, and provides that on an assignment of the reversion, the burden of any condition or covenant entered into by the landlord, having reference to the subject matter of the lease, will run with the reversion.

The tenant's lease

Transmission on the assignment of the lease is covered by the common law rules of privity of estate, going as far back as *Spencer's Case* (1583) 5 Co. Rep. 16a, so that the burden of covenants to be performed by the tenant and the benefit of the covenants to be performed by the landlord will pass to an assignee of the lease if they 'touch and concern' the demised premises. While it is settled that a covenant which has reference to the subject matter of the lease, and one which touches and concerns the demised premises is one and the same thing, the use of different phraseology has always been considered anomalous, and the determination of whether a particular covenant falls within or without the class has often led to litigation.

Further complications in the area of enforceability of leasehold covenants are caused by the application of sections 78 and 79 LPA 1925 which, although intended to relate to the passing of the benefit and burden of covenants relating to freehold land, also appear to operate in relation to leases.

8.1.2 Existing leases

Under existing leases, the landlord will continue to require assignees to covenant directly with the landlord to observe the covenants of the lease. In most cases the lease will stipulate that assignees' direct covenants should endure until the end of the lease term and possibly into any holding over or lease extension.

8.1.3 The new regime

The aim of the new Act is to ensure that the existing blend of common law rules and statutory provisions ceases to apply to new leases, there being created instead a new framework for the transmission of the benefit and burden of covenants contained in leases. Accordingly, by section 30(4) of the Act, the provisions of sections 78 and 79, and sections 141 and 142 LPA 1925 cease to have effect in relation to new leases.

The general effect of the new provisions is that all covenants and obligations between lessor and lessee are enforceable only between the landlord and tenant for the time being. Hence, where the lease or the reversion is assigned, the assignee becomes bound as from the date of the assignment (and until the Act provides him with his release) by the whole package of rights and obligations binding upon his predecessor. The assignee has no liability in respect of any breach of covenant occurring prior to the assignment to him, and the assignor (of the landlord's reversion or of the tenant's lease) has no rights against the other party to the lease as from the date of the assignment by him.

Section 3(1) provides that the benefit and burden of all landlord and tenant covenants of a tenancy shall respectively be annexed and incident to the whole, and to each and every part of the reversion and the demised premises, and that the benefit and burden of such covenants shall, in accordance with section 3, pass on an assignment of the whole or any part.

Under the new law, no distinction is drawn between covenants which 'touch and concern' the demised premises and those which do not, or covenants which 'have reference to the subject matter of the lease', and those which do not. Section 2(1) states that the Act applies to any landlord or tenant covenant of a tenancy whether or not the covenant has reference to the subject matter of the tenancy, and whether the covenant is express, implied or imposed by law.

Under section 28(1), 'covenant' includes a term, condition and obligation. The 'covenant' may be contained in the lease, or in some collateral agreement which under section 28(1) means any agreement collateral to the lease (e.g. deed of variation, side letter, licence to assign), whether made before or after the lease was entered into. These definitions overcome a slight anomaly contained in section 141 LPA 1925 (which refers to covenants and provisions contained in the lease) and section 142 LPA 1925 (which differs by referring to obligations under conditions and covenants entered into by the lessor, whether in the lease or otherwise). An 'assignment' is defined under section 28(1) to include an equitable assignment.

Benefit of covenants

Sections 3(2)(b) and 3(3)(b) provide that, as from an assignment of the reversion by the landlord or an assignment of the lease by the tenant, the assignee becomes entitled, as the case may be, to the benefit of the landlord or the tenant covenants of the lease (except those which fall to be complied with in relation to demised premises not comprised in the assignment). Separate provision is made for the transmission of the benefit of a landlord's right of re entry, since such a right is not in the nature of a covenant or obligation (and therefore falls outside the scope of s 3). Section 4 therefore provides that a landlord's right of re-entry under a tenancy shall be annexed and incident to, and shall pass on an assignment of the whole and each and every part of the reversion.

Burden of covenants

Sections 3(2)(a) and 3(3)(b) provide that as from an assignment of the reversion by the landlord, or an assignment of the lease by the tenant, the assignee becomes bound by those covenants of the lease which bound his predecessor immediately before the assignment (except those which fall to be complied with in relation to demised premises not comprised in the assignment).

It may be the case that, prior to the assignment, the assignor had been given a waiver or release from a particular covenant, which was intended to be personal only, and was not intended to be taken advantage of by a successor in title. Such personal releases can still be given under the new regime because, in determining whether a covenant was binding upon the assignor immediately before the assignment, section 3(4) states that any waiver or release of the covenant which, in whatever terms, is expressed to be personal to the assignor is to be disregarded.

Personal covenants

Of course, some covenants are intended to be personal only, in that, for example, only the original landlord or tenant is intended to be caught by it. The combined effect of sections 2(1) and 3(1) might, unless qualified, have rendered an assignee of the lease bound by such a covenant. Therefore it is provided by section 3(6)(a) that nothing in section 3 shall operate to make a personal covenant (i.e. one which, in whatever terms, is expressed to be personal to any person) enforceable by or, as the case may be, against any other person.

Taking advantage of existing breaches

Enforceability is intended to be between current landlord and current tenant, for breaches occurring during their respective periods of ownership. Section 23(1) provides, therefore, that where as a result of an assignment a person becomes bound by, or entitled to, the benefit of a covenant, he is not to have any liability or rights under the covenant in relation to the period of time before the assignment. At face value, this means that, for example, an assignee of the reversion is not entitled to pursue rent arrears existing at the date of the assignment. The right to pursue those arrears (and damages for other existing breaches) remains with the assignor under section 24(4). However, it was considered necessary to retain the ability of, for example, an assignee of the landlord's reversion to take advantage of existing breaches of covenant (perhaps by purchasing the right to pursue existing rent arrears), and so section 23(2) states that section 23(1) does not preclude the express assignment of such rights.

By contrast (see s 23(3)), where as a result of an assignment of the reversion a person becomes entitled to a right of re-entry, that right is exercisable in relation to both post- and pre-assignment breaches, unless there has been a waiver of the right to forfeit. Were this not the case, a right to forfeit for a once and for all breach of covenant by the tenant would be lost by an assignment of the reversion.

Effect of a release

Release from a covenant under the Act brings liability under that covenant to an end. However, it does not affect liability for any breach of covenant committed before the release (see s 24(1)), and, naturally, where an assigning

tenant or landlord fails to obtain a release under the Act, the assignment by
him does not affect his continuing liability (see s 24(3)).

Surety covenants

The new provisions relate only to transmission of the benefit and burden of
covenants entered into by the landlord and tenant under the lease, and not
by a third party, such as a guarantor or a management company.

Under the existing law, on an assignment of the landlord's reversion, the
benefit of a guarantor's covenant passes to the assignee of the reversion.
This is not under section 141(1) **LPA** 1925, but under the common law rule
that the assignee has the legal estate vested in him, and the covenant touches
and concerns the legal estate. (See *P & A Swift Investments v Combined English
Stores Group plc* [1989] AC 643.) The basic rule of 'touching and concerning'
has not been abolished by the new legislation. However, as mentioned
above, the rule has been altered insofar as it applies to landlord and tenant
covenants.

Management covenants

As regards management covenants, section 12(2) provides that, to the extent
that a covenant in the lease confers a right against a third party such as a
management company (e.g. to maintain common parts, perform services,
etc.), then, for the purpose of transmitting the benefit of that covenant, if
the right is exercisable by the tenant, the covenant is to be treated as a
landlord covenant of the tenancy (enabling the tenant's successors to sue if
services are not provided), and if the right is exercisable by the landlord, the
covenant is to be treated as if it were a tenant covenant of the tenancy.

Similarly, where a covenant grants a right to the third party (e.g. to
receive service charge payments) then, for the purpose of transmitting the
burden of that covenant (and, indeed, for the purpose of providing to the
other party a release under the Act from that covenant), if the right is
exercisable against the tenant, the covenant is to be treated as if it were a

tenant covenant (so that the tenant may be released on assignment under section 5 and his successor takes the burden under section 3(2)(a)), and, in the less likely event of the covenant being exercisable against the landlord, it is to be treated as a landlord covenant.

The ability of a mortgagee in possession of the reversion to take advantage of the tenant covenants is preserved by section 15, which also enables a tenant's mortgagee in possession to pursue a defaulting landlord.

8.2 ASSIGNING PART

On an assignment of part to which section 5 applies, the tenant will be released from his covenants to the extent that they fall to be complied with in relation to the part assigned. He therefore remains liable on those covenants which fall to be complied with in relation to the premises he retains, and covenants which are not attributable to any particular part of the demised premises. The corollary of those propositions is that the assignee becomes bound by the tenant covenants of the tenancy, except personal covenants and those covenants which fall to be complied with in relation to the premises retained by the tenant. Those which are non-attributable are also binding upon the assignee.

A covenant which falls to be complied in relation to a particular part of the premises comprised in a lease is defined by section 28(2) as:

- one which, in its terms, applies to that part of the premises; or
- one which in its practical application can be attributed to that part (even if it can also be attributed to other parts of the premises).

On this basis, the usual leasehold covenants such as a covenant to repair, a user covenant or a covenant against subletting would fall within the definition since, in a practical application, they can be attributed to the part assigned, even though they can also be attributed to the part retained. By section 28(3), covenants which involve the payment of money (e.g. covenants to pay rent, service charge, insurance premiums) fall outside the definition, unless the covenant in terms applies to that part, or the amount of the payment is determined specifically by reference to that part or by anything falling to be done by the occupier of that part. Therefore, covenants to pay money will not usually be covenants which fall to be complied with in relation to any particular part of premises. They are the 'non-attributable' covenants referred to above and in sections 9 and 10 of the Act.

If the tenant has not been released from a non-attributable covenant but the assignee has also become bound by it, then they are bound by it jointly and severally under section 13(1). However, by virtue of section 9(1), the tenant and assignee can agree to apportion their liability in such manner as they see fit (even to the extent that one party is exonerated from all liability). Procedures exist under section 10 to make such an apportionment binding upon the landlord of the whole of the demised premises (or if the reversion is severed, the several landlords), by way of written notice to the landlord in prescribed form within four weeks after the assignment. The apportionment will become binding on the landlord if he does not object to the notice within four weeks of service upon him, or, where he does object, if the county court makes a declaration that it is reasonable for the apportionment to become binding upon him.

Similar rules exist under sections 9 and 10 for the apportionment of liability under covenants on the assignment of part of the reversion.

8.3 FORFEITURE AND DISCLAIMER AS TO PART

A certain amount of tidying up has been done in relation to new leases in the area of forfeiture, and disclaimer by liquidators and trustees in bankruptcy. Under section 21(1), where by virtue of an assignment a tenant is the tenant of part only of the premises demised by the lease, but there is a proviso for re-entry relating to the whole of the premises, a breach of covenant by the tenant will only entitle the landlord to forfeit the tenant's part. Under section 21(2), where again the tenant has become a tenant of part only of premises demised by the lease, disclaimer by his liquidator or trustee in bankruptcy will only relate to that part.

8.4 VARIOUS SAVINGS

Nothing in the Act affects:

- covenants under sections 35 and 155 of the Housing Act 1985, which relate to the repayment of discounts to local authorities following an early disposal of property by a former council tenant;
- covenants under paragraph 1 of schedule 6A of the Housing Act 1985 relating to the redemption of the landlord's share in the case of shared equity council house purchases;
- covenants under paragraph 1 or 3 of schedule 2 of the Housing Associations Act 1985 relating to the repayment of discounts provided to purchasers from Housing Associations on an early disposal, and certain restrictions on disposal of former Housing Association properties; or
- the operation of section 3(3A) of the Landlord and Tenant Act 1985, which preserves the liability of a former landlord until the tenant has been notified of the new landlord's name and address.

8.5 VARIOUS REPEALS

As has been seen at 8.1.3, sections 78 and 79 and sections 141 and 142 LPA 1925 cease to apply in relation to new leases. One consequence of the abolition of privity of contract which should not be overlooked is that an indemnity covenant on the assignment of a new lease is not required. Accordingly, as regards new leases sections 77(1)(C) and 77(1)(D) LPA 1925, and sections 24(1)(b) and 24(2) LRA 1925 are repealed. These repeals do not preclude a former tenant who is liable under an AGA from obtaining an indemnity from his assignee either expressly in the deed of assignment or by implication under the law of suretyship.

A PRACTITIONER'S VIEW

The transmission of the benefit and burden

The amendments have simplified and codified the rules relating to the transmission of the benefit and burden of leasehold covenants in respect of new leases. The following points briefly summarise the position of landlord and tenant under such a lease.

▷A landlord:
- can sue his tenant for breaches of tenant covenants committed while he is the landlord;
- cannot sue for breaches committed before he became the landlord, unless he takes an assignment of the right to sue;
- can forfeit for breaches committed before he became the landlord, unless the right to forfeit has been lost;
- can sue after he has parted with the reversion, for breaches committed while he was the landlord, unless he has assigned the right to sue;
- can be sued at any time for breaches he commits from the time he became the landlord until the date he obtains his release;
- can sue any guarantor under a guarantee even though the reversion may have changed hands.

▷A tenant:
- can sue his landlord for breaches of landlord covenants committed while he is the tenant;
- cannot sue for breaches committed before he became the tenant, unless he takes an assignment of the right to sue;
- can be sued at any time for breaches he commits from the time he became the tenant until the date he obtains his release;
- can sue a management company under its covenants as if those covenants were landlord covenants.

effect on the workings of the property market

9.1 CAPITAL VALUES

9.1.1 Timing of the legislation

Most landlords acknowledge, to a greater or lesser extent, the inequity of an original tenant being liable for the misdemeanours of an assignee (perhaps once or twice removed). Unfortunately, Parliament chose, as far as property investors were concerned, the worst possible period—the early 1990s—to attempt to introduce legislation limiting privity of contract for commercial leases. The impetus may have been a desire to protect assignors from assignee default during the economic recession, but the various proposals also coincided with the deepest commercial property recession since the war. In the event, the various Bills took so long to culminate in the Act that the economic recession had long since ended (although some individuals may have difficulty in accepting this statement) and the rate of tenant default has now been falling for some time.

In contrast, the 1988 Law Commission's report was produced at a time when interest in the subject of privity of contract could hardly have been lower. At that time, landlords/investors were often only too delighted to secure vacant possession by forfeiture or otherwise terminating the lease, so as to relet the property at a higher rent or to undertake development or refurbishment. Companies were generally expanding and tenant default was unusual.

Since the beginning of the 1990s, however, very little rental growth has been evident in the market. Worse than that, many properties have seen their rental values fall over the past five years—in some instances to less than half of their late 1980s value. The capital values of these properties have come, in particular, to rely heavily on the provisions of the typical institutional lease which ensures that the rent cannot fall at review and also on the covenant of the tenant or his predecessor in title.

Without such protection, investors' suffering in the property recession would have been greater. It is therefore not surprising that, despite the sympathy that many of them felt towards smaller tenants (particularly those individuals not in business any more), they were very reluctant to give up their historic rights. An even greater initial worry was, of course, that legislation might, to some extent, have been retrospective, possibly removing privity of contract for all leases, whether new or existing. In no small part due to the lobbying by various bodies representing landlords' and investors' interests, the final form of legislation represented a generally acceptable compromise.

Underlying this is the expectation by investors that there will not, in the foreseeable future, be a repeat of the falls in rental values which have occurred in the last five years and the properties which experienced a loss in value at the time were, by definition, let on pre-legislation leases and are therefore unaffected. (Those properties which either were unlet or had their leases expire at an untimely point could not benefit from privity of contract anyway.)

What should be clear from the above paragraphs is that the effect of abolition of privity of contract varies depending upon the state of the property market. When optimistic sentiments prevail, security of income becomes a low priority and, conversely, when a recession occurs, investors look towards the contractual obligations contained in the lease to ensure that, at least, their income is unaffected.

Currently, there is a degree of mixed sentiments. Investors are looking forward to a period of rising rental values, but they also recognise that the risks of not achieving such growth are exceptionally high. Nevertheless, it is likely that we are entering a period when the market increasingly focuses on growth and the gradual erosion of the security of income occasioned by the transition of leases under the Act is not explicitly acknowledged in market pricing. In effect, other factors of performance and risk will tend to dominate until, of course, the next down-phase occurs and the market, once again, focuses its attention on the income characteristics of property.

9.1.2 Effect on the market as a whole

While investors were concerned about the impact on individual properties, many institutions (insurance companies and pension funds) were also very concerned about the effect of the Act on perceptions of overall values in the property market. Like all investments, the value of property reflects both the expectation of returns and the risks that such returns may not be achieved. Thus, the abolition of privity of contract can alter this relationship increasing the financial loss associated with tenant default and, consequently, the value of property should fall to reflect this. As, however, the legislation only affects new leases in this respect, the effect will be gradual and spread over a long period. It will probably take in the region of ten years before the majority of occupational leases are new leases and perhaps another ten years before the market consists overwhelmingly of such leases.

Institutional investors are not, of course, the only major players in the market. Property companies (quoted or private) and high net-worth individuals also play a part and sometimes their role can be quite substantial. The big difference between the two groups is in the method of financing their investments. The institutions will almost exclusively use equity finance, whereas the property companies/individuals will use a greater or lesser proportion of debt finance. The debt is typically provided by domestic or foreign banks and their position is somewhat different. They are lending money at a margin to produce a profit; the margin may reflect the degree of risk involved in the transaction, but basically the cost of money is priced on the expectation that the principal will be returned in due course. They have little concern about growth in value—their interest is in ensuring that adequate security for the debt is provided. For them, therefore, anything which erodes that security needs to be taken seriously. Already during the period when abolition of privity of contract was under discussion, many banks showed themselves reluctant to advance monies where the covenant strength of an original tenant formed part of the security—because of the risk of retrospective legislation.

Now that the position is clearer, they will need to consider what controls the landlord is able to exercise in the event of an application to assign to a weaker covenant (and even the affect of a further assignment) so as to protect the quality of the income flow. This might, ultimately, prove to be the most significant effect on property values.

9.1.3 New provisions

Of course, the Act also provides for landlords to have a greater degree of control over the assignee than previously. These controls can take the form of an AGA by the assignor (subject to the sort of conditions explained in chapter 3), and lease provisions pre-determining the acceptability of the assignee. Together, these provisions go some way towards mitigating the effects of the abolition of privity of contract. Indeed, it is not inconceivable that, should the bargaining strengths of the respective parties change, the Act may place landlords in a stronger position than they might otherwise be.

9.1.4 Differential effects

Although it is suggested that the overall effect on the market will be muted because of the time-scale involved there will, nevertheless, be some parts of the market more adversely affected than others.

For most of the past 30 or so years, investors have held property as, essentially, an equity-type investment. In other words, they are holding the assets not just for their current income but also because of their growth prospects. For such investments, the security of income comes secondary to the growth prospects. Indeed, if the investment is truly one which does grow in value, it is because there is increasing occupational demand for it and, in the event of tenant default, a re-letting should therefore be readily achievable.

Such an argument applies to a lesser extent to those properties which are producing higher income (relative to their value), because their growth prospects are perceived to be limited. Typically, such properties are older obsolete industrial buildings, although retail and office properties can also fall into this category. It might be thought that such properties would be those most affected by the legislation but, of course, these properties will be let on leases which were granted prior to the implementation of the Act and will therefore not be affected.

The above arguments do, however, point to the type of property investment which will be most adversely affected by the legislation. These are properties which are obsolescent—in other words, those which tend to become obsolete. Obsolescence can be physical in nature, where the building fabric and services are no longer able to fulfil their intended purpose, or economic where the location, size, layout, etc. mean that the building can no longer be used for a purpose which is financially viable. Of all the commercial property sectors, offices have shown the highest level of historic obsolescence although industrial properties also exhibit this characteristic.

Retail properties, partly as a result of relatively tight planning policies, but also because a large part of their value is due to the location, have not been so prone, but the greater proliferation of alternative retailing types and locations is expected to mean that obsolescence will become a more important factor for this group in the future. Although it is difficult to generalise in respect of the life of a building, locations which are located marginally to central areas and building types which tend to be specialised in their design would normally be expected to be most at risk.

9.2 LEASE PROVISIONS AND RENTAL VALUES
9.2.1 Lease negotiations

Although the Act is not expected to come into effect until 1 January 1996, it has already started to become a factor in negotiations for new leases. In open market lettings, prospective tenants (who are currently in a strong negotiating position) are, in some instances, requiring the lease to contain provisions which are designed to provide the benefit to tenants that the Act provides. Most tenants, however, believe that, as they are currently able to negotiate either short leases or leases with break clauses, they are provided with sufficient ability to avoid future problems with privity of contract. Of course, over time, the balance of power will swing back toward landlords but then the new leases will fall within the Act's provisions.

Although, in future, landlords will have the ability to require an AGA in respect of the immediate assignee and/or predetermine the acceptability of the assignee, no 'Institutional Standard Clauses' are available and we will undoubtedly see a period when various versions vie for universal acceptance. Perhaps the greatest difficulty in this respect will be the form that the test for assignees' acceptability will take. A rule of thumb that some landlords have applied in the past is that a prospective tenant's or assignee's net profit should be equal to at least three times the rent on the building to be occupied. The flaws in such a measure are, unfortunately, all too obvious. Nevertheless, it is likely that an acceptable explicit test will tend to focus on the financial position of the assignee and will need to be quite precise in its application. Measures such as those used in assessing credit ratings and corporate bond qualities would seem to have much application in this area.

9.2.2 Market rent

Arguably, there could be a difference between the rent which a tenant is willing to pay under a new lease, where privity of contract is excluded, and an existing lease, where privity of contract still continues.

In practice, the situation is more likely to be akin to the arguments sometimes put forward that tenants would be willing to pay higher rents for a shorter lease on the basis that these limited their privity liabilities. Unfortunately, the evidence for supporting such a case has always been very scant and it is only in particular situations that a landlord has been able to succeed before an arbitrator at a rent review. In general, market inefficiencies and different tenant perceptions make it difficult to differentiate the 'premium' that a tenant might be willing to pay for the exclusion of privity of contract.

This is not to say, however, that it may not occur in future. With a growing number of leases from which privity of contract has been excluded, sufficient evidence may develop to differentiate a privity effect.

There is, nevertheless, one further complication. Although, traditionally, 'institutional-type' leases have been of twenty-five years length, this practice has substantially changed for leases granted since the beginning of the 1990s. More typically now, lease lengths are between five and fifteen years, with most of these longer terms also incorporating tenant's or mutual break clauses (sometimes, admittedly, with penalties) and, for such leases, the tenant's liabilities for privity of contract are obviously very much lower.

Indeed, it could be argued that, from the perspective of tenants, the abolition of privity of contract currently will have little effect because their negotiating strength in the market place ensures that they can secure most of the benefits anyway.

9.2.3 Rent reviews

Landlords need to be conscious that if they are able to impose conditions on assignment which are unusually onerous, these are likely to be picked up by the tenant or his surveyor during the rent review process and used in negotiations. The tenant will typically argue a case that, on the basis of the comparable evidence of market rents, the subject property is less attractive to a tenant because of the difficulties which will be experienced in finding a suitable assignee, and, therefore, the reviewed rent should reflect this.

This might become a particular issue over the next few years, as existing leases would normally contain no provisions limiting assignments (other than requiring the landlord's consent, which is not to be unreasonably withheld), and as these normally form at least a part of comparable rental evidence, conceivably a case may be made in respect of any provision which is more restrictive than the previous norm.

9.3 ESTATE MANAGEMENT

Although solicitors will only occasionally become involved in issues of day-to-day estate management, it is worth considering how the Act may affect working practices.

Perhaps the most important aspect in this area relates to the ability of the landlord to recover arrears of rent and service charges from the assignor/tenant. The Act, in requiring a default notice to be served within six months of the date when the amount was due (see chapter 5), places an onus on the landlord to take action at a relatively early stage. Because there may be difficulties in tracing the whereabouts of the former tenant and ensuring that the notice is correctly served, this might suggest that action needs to be taken when, say, the rent is only three months in arrears. At this point, the landlord might normally still be pursuing the existing tenant and only when all normal action has been exhausted would he then look toward a previous tenant. This also suggests a requirement for landlords/agents to maintain adequate records and systems to prompt this action.

Even serving such a notice is not, however, without its downside. The ability of the recipient to respond with the right to call for an overriding lease means that the landlord should reflect on the effect of such an outcome if the recipient does so (see chapter 6).

Finally, the landlord's ability to secure a release from his own covenants on disposal on a property is a new concept. In the frenzy of a sale, this issue is something which may very easily be overlooked.

Landlord and Tenant (Covenants) Act 1995

CHAPTER 30

ARRANGEMENT OF SECTIONS

Landlord and Tenant (Covenants) Act 1995

1995 CHAPTER 30

An Act to make provision for persons bound by covenants of a tenancy to be released from such covenants on the assignment of the tenancy, and to make other provision with respect to rights and liabilities arising under such covenants; to restrict in certain circumstances the operation of rights of re-entry, forfeiture and disclaimer; and for connected purposes. [19th July 1995]

B E IT ENACTED by the Queen's most Excellent Majesty, by and with the advice and consent of the Lords Spiritual and Temporal, and Commons, in this present Parliament assembled, and by the authority of the same, as follows:—

Preliminary

1.—(1) Sections 3 to 16 and 21 apply only to new tenancies.

Tenancies to which the Act applies.

(2) Sections 17 to 20 apply to both new and other tenancies.

(3) For the purposes of this section a tenancy is a new tenancy if it is granted on or after the date on which this Act comes into force otherwise than in pursuance of—

(a) an agreement entered into before that date, or

(b) an order of a court made before that date.

(4) Subsection (3) has effect subject to section 20(1) in the case of overriding leases granted under section 19.

(5) Without prejudice to the generality of subsection (3), that subsection applies to the grant of a tenancy where by virtue of any variation of a tenancy there is a deemed surrender and regrant as it applies to any other grant of a tenancy.

(6) Where a tenancy granted on or after the date on which this Act comes into force is so granted in pursuance of an option granted before that date, the tenancy shall be regarded for the purposes of subsection (3)

as granted in pursuance of an agreement entered into before that date (and accordingly is not a new tenancy), whether or not the option was exercised before that date.

(7) In subsection (6) "option" includes right of first refusal.

Covenants to which the Act applies.

2.—(1) This Act applies to a landlord covenant or a tenant covenant of a tenancy—

(a) whether or not the covenant has reference to the subject matter of the tenancy, and

(b) whether the covenant is express, implied or imposed by law,

but does not apply to a covenant falling within subsection (2).

(2) Nothing in this Act affects any covenant imposed in pursuance of—

1985 c. 68.

(a) section 35 or 155 of the Housing Act 1985 (covenants for repayment of discount on early disposals);

(b) paragraph 1 of Schedule 6A to that Act (covenants requiring redemption of landlord's share); or

1985 c. 69.

(c) paragraph 1 or 3 of Schedule 2 to the Housing Associations Act 1985 (covenants for repayment of discount on early disposals or for restricting disposals).

Transmission of covenants

Transmission of benefit and burden of covenants.

3.—(1) The benefit and burden of all landlord and tenant covenants of a tenancy—

(a) shall be annexed and incident to the whole, and to each and every part, of the premises demised by the tenancy and of the reversion in them, and

(b) shall in accordance with this section pass on an assignment of the whole or any part of those premises or of the reversion in them.

(2) Where the assignment is by the tenant under the tenancy, then as from the assignment the assignee—

(a) becomes bound by the tenant covenants of the tenancy except to the extent that—

(i) immediately before the assignment they did not bind the assignor, or

(ii) they fall to be complied with in relation to any demised premises not comprised in the assignment; and

(b) becomes entitled to the benefit of the landlord covenants of the tenancy except to the extent that they fall to be complied with in relation to any such premises.

(3) Where the assignment is by the landlord under the tenancy, then as from the assignment the assignee—

(a) becomes bound by the landlord covenants of the tenancy except to the extent that—

(i) immediately before the assignment they did not bind the assignor, or

(ii) they fall to be complied with in relation to any demised premises not comprised in the assignment; and

(b) becomes entitled to the benefit of the tenant covenants of the tenancy except to the extent that they fall to be complied with in relation to any such premises.

(4) In determining for the purposes of subsection (2) or (3) whether any covenant bound the assignor immediately before the assignment, any waiver or release of the covenant which (in whatever terms) is expressed to be personal to the assignor shall be disregarded.

(5) Any landlord or tenant covenant of a tenancy which is restrictive of the user of land shall, as well as being capable of enforcement against an assignee, be capable of being enforced against any other person who is the owner or occupier of any demised premises to which the covenant relates, even though there is no express provision in the tenancy to that effect.

(6) Nothing in this section shall operate—

(a) in the case of a covenant which (in whatever terms) is expressed to be personal to any person, to make the covenant enforceable by or (as the case may be) against any other person; or

(b) to make a covenant enforceable against any person if, apart from this section, it would not be enforceable against him by reason of its not having been registered under the Land Registration Act 1925 or the Land Charges Act 1972.

1925 c. 21.
1972 c. 61.

(7) To the extent that there remains in force any rule of law by virtue of which the burden of a covenant whose subject matter is not in existence at the time when it is made does not run with the land affected unless the covenantor covenants on behalf of himself and his assigns, that rule of law is hereby abolished in relation to tenancies.

4. The benefit of a landlord's right of re-entry under a tenancy—

Transmission of rights of re-entry.

(a) shall be annexed and incident to the whole, and to each and every part, of the reversion in the premises demised by the tenancy, and

(b) shall pass on an assignment of the whole or any part of the reversion in those premises.

Release of covenants on assignment

5.—(1) This section applies where a tenant assigns premises demised to him under a tenancy.

Tenant released from covenants on assignment of tenancy.

(2) If the tenant assigns the whole of the premises demised to him, he—

(a) is released from the tenant covenants of the tenancy, and

(b) ceases to be entitled to the benefit of the landlord covenants of the tenancy,

as from the assignment.

(3) If the tenant assigns part only of the premises demised to him, then as from the assignment he—

(a) is released from the tenant covenants of the tenancy, and

(b) ceases to be entitled to the benefit of the landlord covenants of the tenancy,

only to the extent that those covenants fall to be complied with in relation to that part of the demised premises.

(4) This section applies as mentioned in subsection (1) whether or not the tenant is tenant of the whole of the premises comprised in the tenancy.

Landlord may be released from covenants on assignment of reversion.

6.—(1) This section applies where a landlord assigns the reversion in premises of which he is the landlord under a tenancy.

(2) If the landlord assigns the reversion in the whole of the premises of which he is the landlord—

    (a) he may apply to be released from the landlord covenants of the tenancy in accordance with section 8; and

    (b) if he is so released from all of those covenants, he ceases to be entitled to the benefit of the tenant covenants of the tenancy as from the assignment.

(3) If the landlord assigns the reversion in part only of the premises of which he is the landlord—

    (a) he may apply to be so released from the landlord covenants of the tenancy to the extent that they fall to be complied with in relation to that part of those premises; and

    (b) if he is, to that extent, so released from all of those covenants, then as from the assignment he ceases to be entitled to the benefit of the tenant covenants only to the extent that they fall to be complied with in relation to that part of those premises.

(4) This section applies as mentioned in subsection (1) whether or not the landlord is landlord of the whole of the premises comprised in the tenancy.

Former landlord may be released from covenants on assignment of reversion.

7.—(1) This section applies where—

    (a) a landlord assigns the reversion in premises of which he is the landlord under a tenancy, and

    (b) immediately before the assignment a former landlord of the premises remains bound by a landlord covenant of the tenancy ("the relevant covenant").

(2) If immediately before the assignment the former landlord does not remain the landlord of any other premises demised by the tenancy, he may apply to be released from the relevant covenant in accordance with section 8.

(3) In any other case the former landlord may apply to be so released from the relevant covenant to the extent that it falls to be complied with in relation to any premises comprised in the assignment.

(4) If the former landlord is so released from every landlord covenant by which he remained bound immediately before the assignment, he ceases to be entitled to the benefit of the tenant covenants of the tenancy.

(5) If the former landlord is so released from every such landlord covenant to the extent that it falls to be complied with in relation to any premises comprised in the assignment, he ceases to be entitled to the benefit of the tenant covenants of the tenancy to the extent that they fall to be so complied with.

(6) This section applies as mentioned in subsection (1)—

    (a) whether or not the landlord making the assignment is landlord of the whole of the premises comprised in the tenancy; and

(b) whether or not the former landlord has previously applied (whether under section 6 or this section) to be released from the relevant covenant.

8.—(1) For the purposes of section 6 or 7 an application for the release of a covenant to any extent is made by serving on the tenant, either before or within the period of four weeks beginning with the date of the assignment in question, a notice informing him of—

Procedure for seeking release from a covenant under section 6 or 7.

(a) the proposed assignment or (as the case may be) the fact that the assignment has taken place, and

(b) the request for the covenant to be released to that extent.

(2) Where an application for the release of a covenant is made in accordance with subsection (1), the covenant is released to the extent mentioned in the notice if—

(a) the tenant does not, within the period of four weeks beginning with the day on which the notice is served, serve on the landlord or former landlord a notice in writing objecting to the release, or

(b) the tenant does so serve such a notice but the court, on the application of the landlord or former landlord, makes a declaration that it is reasonable for the covenant to be so released, or

(c) the tenant serves on the landlord or former landlord a notice in writing consenting to the release and, if he has previously served a notice objecting to it, stating that that notice is withdrawn.

(3) Any release from a covenant in accordance with this section shall be regarded as occurring at the time when the assignment in question takes place.

(4) In this section—

(a) "the tenant" means the tenant of the premises comprised in the assignment in question (or, if different parts of those premises are held under the tenancy by different tenants, each of those tenants);

(b) any reference to the landlord or the former landlord is a reference to the landlord referred to in section 6 or the former landlord referred to in section 7, as the case may be; and

(c) "the court" means a county court.

Apportionment of liability between assignor and assignee

9.—(1) This section applies where—

(a) a tenant assigns part only of the premises demised to him by a tenancy;

Apportionment of liability under covenants binding both assignor and assignee of tenancy or reversion.

(b) after the assignment both the tenant and his assignee are to be bound by a non-attributable tenant covenant of the tenancy; and

(c) the tenant and his assignee agree that as from the assignment liability under the covenant is to be apportioned between them in such manner as is specified in the agreement.

(2) This section also applies where—

(a) a landlord assigns the reversion in part only of the premises of which he is the landlord under a tenancy;

(b) after the assignment both the landlord and his assignee are to be bound by a non-attributable landlord covenant of the tenancy; and

(c) the landlord and his assignee agree that as from the assignment liability under the covenant is to be apportioned between them in such manner as is specified in the agreement.

(3) Any such agreement as is mentioned in subsection (1) or (2) may apportion liability in such a way that a party to the agreement is exonerated from all liability under a covenant.

(4) In any case falling within subsection (1) or (2) the parties to the agreement may apply for the apportionment to become binding on the appropriate person in accordance with section 10.

(5) In any such case the parties to the agreement may also apply for the apportionment to become binding on any person (other than the appropriate person) who is for the time being entitled to enforce the covenant in question; and section 10 shall apply in relation to such an application as it applies in relation to an application made with respect to the appropriate person.

(6) For the purposes of this section a covenant is, in relation to an assignment, a "non-attributable" covenant if it does not fall to be complied with in relation to any premises comprised in the assignment.

(7) In this section "the appropriate person" means either—

(a) the landlord of the entire premises referred to in subsection (1)(a) (or, if different parts of those premises are held under the tenancy by different landlords, each of those landlords), or

(b) the tenant of the entire premises referred to in subsection (2)(a) (or, if different parts of those premises are held under the tenancy by different tenants, each of those tenants),

depending on whether the agreement in question falls within subsection (1) or subsection (2).

Procedure for making apportionment bind other party to lease.

10.—(1) For the purposes of section 9 the parties to an agreement falling within subsection (1) or (2) of that section apply for an apportionment to become binding on the appropriate person if, either before or within the period of four weeks beginning with the date of the assignment in question, they serve on that person a notice informing him of—

(a) the proposed assignment or (as the case may be) the fact that the assignment has taken place;

(b) the prescribed particulars of the agreement; and

(c) their request that the apportionment should become binding on him.

(2) Where an application for an apportionment to become binding has been made in accordance with subsection (1), the apportionment becomes binding on the appropriate person if—

(a) he does not, within the period of four weeks beginning with the day on which the notice is served under subsection (1), serve on the parties to the agreement a notice in writing objecting to the apportionment becoming binding on him, or

(b) he does so serve such a notice but the court, on the application of the parties to the agreement, makes a declaration that it is reasonable for the apportionment to become binding on him, or

(c) he serves on the parties to the agreement a notice in writing consenting to the apportionment becoming binding on him and, if he has previously served a notice objecting thereto, stating that that notice is withdrawn.

(3) Where any apportionment becomes binding in accordance with this section, this shall be regarded as occurring at the time when the assignment in question takes place.

(4) In this section—

"the appropriate person" has the same meaning as in section 9;

"the court" means a county court;

"prescribed" means prescribed by virtue of section 27.

Excluded assignments

11.—(1) This section provides for the operation of sections 5 to 10 in relation to assignments in breach of a covenant of a tenancy or assignments by operation of law ("excluded assignments"). *Assignments in breach of covenant or by operation of law.*

(2) In the case of an excluded assignment subsection (2) or (3) of section 5—

(a) shall not have the effect mentioned in that subsection in relation to the tenant as from that assignment, but

(b) shall have that effect as from the next assignment (if any) of the premises assigned by him which is not an excluded assignment.

(3) In the case of an excluded assignment subsection (2) or (3) of section 6 or 7—

(a) shall not enable the landlord or former landlord to apply for such a release as is mentioned in that subsection as from that assignment, but

(b) shall apply on the next assignment (if any) of the reversion assigned by the landlord which is not an excluded assignment so as to enable the landlord or former landlord to apply for any such release as from that subsequent assignment.

(4) Where subsection (2) or (3) of section 6 or 7 does so apply—

(a) any reference in that section to the assignment (except where it relates to the time as from which the release takes effect) is a reference to the excluded assignment; but

(b) in that excepted case and in section 8 as it applies in relation to any application under that section made by virtue of subsection (3) above, any reference to the assignment or proposed assignment is a reference to any such subsequent assignment as is mentioned in that subsection.

(5) In the case of an excluded assignment section 9—

    (a) shall not enable the tenant or landlord and his assignee to apply for an agreed apportionment to become binding in accordance with section 10 as from that assignment, but

    (b) shall apply on the next assignment (if any) of the premises or reversion assigned by the tenant or landlord which is not an excluded assignment so as to enable him and his assignee to apply for such an apportionment to become binding in accordance with section 10 as from that subsequent assignment.

(6) Where section 9 does so apply—

    (a) any reference in that section to the assignment or the assignee under it is a reference to the excluded assignment and the assignee under that assignment; but

    (b) in section 10 as it applies in relation to any application under section 9 made by virtue of subsection (5) above, any reference to the assignment or proposed assignment is a reference to any such subsequent assignment as is mentioned in that subsection.

(7) If any such subsequent assignment as is mentioned in subsection (2), (3) or (5) above comprises only part of the premises assigned by the tenant or (as the case may be) only part of the premises the reversion in which was assigned by the landlord on the excluded assignment—

    (a) the relevant provision or provisions of section 5, 6, 7 or 9 shall only have the effect mentioned in that subsection to the extent that the covenants or covenant in question fall or falls to be complied with in relation to that part of those premises; and

    (b) that subsection may accordingly apply on different occasions in relation to different parts of those premises.

Third party covenants

Covenants with management companies etc.

12.—(1) This section applies where—

    (a) a person other than the landlord or tenant ("the third party") is under a covenant of a tenancy liable (as principal) to discharge any function with respect to all or any of the demised premises ("the relevant function"); and

    (b) that liability is not the liability of a guarantor or any other financial liability referable to the performance or otherwise of a covenant of the tenancy by another party to it.

(2) To the extent that any covenant of the tenancy confers any rights against the third party with respect to the relevant function, then for the purposes of the transmission of the benefit of the covenant in accordance with this Act it shall be treated as if it were—

    (a) a tenant covenant of the tenancy to the extent that those rights are exercisable by the landlord; and

    (b) a landlord covenant of the tenancy to the extent that those rights are exercisable by the tenant.

(3) To the extent that any covenant of the tenancy confers any rights exercisable by the third party with respect to the relevant function, then for the purposes mentioned in subsection (4), it shall be treated as if it were—

    (a) a tenant covenant of the tenancy to the extent that those rights are exercisable against the tenant; and

    (b) a landlord covenant of the tenancy to the extent that those rights are exercisable against the landlord.

(4) The purposes mentioned in subsection (3) are—

    (a) the transmission of the burden of the covenant in accordance with this Act; and

    (b) any release from, or apportionment of liability in respect of, the covenant in accordance with this Act.

(5) In relation to the release of the landlord from any covenant which is to be treated as a landlord covenant by virtue of subsection (3), section 8 shall apply as if any reference to the tenant were a reference to the third party.

Joint liability under covenants

13.—(1) Where in consequence of this Act two or more persons are bound by the same covenant, they are so bound both jointly and severally.

Covenants binding two or more persons.

(2) Subject to section 24(2), where by virtue of this Act—

    (a) two or more persons are bound jointly and severally by the same covenant, and

    (b) any of the persons so bound is released from the covenant.

the release does not extend to any other of those persons.

(3) For the purpose of providing for contribution between persons who, by virtue of this Act, are bound jointly and severally by a covenant, the Civil Liability (Contribution) Act 1978 shall have effect as if—

1978 c. 47.

    (a) liability to a person under a covenant were liability in respect of damage suffered by that person;

    (b) references to damage accordingly included a breach of a covenant of a tenancy; and

    (c) section 7(2) of that Act were omitted.

14. The following provisions (by virtue of which indemnity covenants are implied on the assignment of a tenancy) shall cease to have effect—

Abolition of indemnity covenants implied by statute.

    (a) subsections (1)(C) and (D) of section 77 of the Law of Property Act 1925; and

1925 c. 20.

    (b) subsections (1)(b) and (2) of section 24 of the Land Registration Act 1925.

1925 c. 21.

Enforcement of covenants

15.—(1) Where any tenant covenant of a tenancy, or any right of re-entry contained in a tenancy, is enforceable by the reversioner in respect of any premises demised by the tenancy, it shall also be so enforceable by—

Enforcement of covenants.

    (a) any person (other than the reversioner) who, as the holder of the immediate reversion in those premises, is for the time being entitled to the rents and profits under the tenancy in respect of those premises, or

(b) any mortgagee in possession of the reversion in those premises who is so entitled.

(2) Where any landlord covenant of a tenancy is enforceable against the reversioner in respect of any premises demised by the tenancy, it shall also be so enforceable against any person falling within subsection (1)(a) or (b).

(3) Where any landlord covenant of a tenancy is enforceable by the tenant in respect of any premises demised by the tenancy, it shall also be so enforceable by any mortgagee in possession of those premises under a mortgage granted by the tenant.

(4) Where any tenant covenant of a tenancy, or any right of re-entry contained in a tenancy, is enforceable against the tenant in respect of any premises demised by the tenancy, it shall also be so enforceable against any such mortgagee.

(5) Nothing in this section shall operate—

(a) in the case of a covenant which (in whatever terms) is expressed to be personal to any person, to make the covenant enforceable by or (as the case may be) against any other person; or

(b) to make a covenant enforceable against any person if, apart from this section, it would not be enforceable against him by reason of its not having been registered under the Land Registration Act 1925 or the Land Charges Act 1972.

1925 c. 21.
1972 c. 61.

(6) In this section—

"mortgagee" and "mortgage" include "chargee" and "charge" respectively;

"the reversioner", in relation to a tenancy, means the holder for the time being of the interest of the landlord under the tenancy.

Liability of former tenant etc. in respect of covenants

Tenant guaranteeing performance of covenant by assignee.

16.—(1) Where on an assignment a tenant is to any extent released from a tenant covenant of a tenancy by virtue of this Act ("the relevant covenant"), nothing in this Act (and in particular section 25) shall preclude him from entering into an authorised guarantee agreement with respect to the performance of that covenant by the assignee.

(2) For the purposes of this section an agreement is an authorised guarantee agreement if—

(a) under it the tenant guarantees the performance of the relevant covenant to any extent by the assignee; and

(b) it is entered into in the circumstances set out in subsection (3); and

(c) its provisions conform with subsections (4) and (5).

(3) Those circumstances are as follows—

(a) by virtue of a covenant against assignment (whether absolute or qualified) the assignment cannot be effected without the consent of the landlord under the tenancy or some other person;

(b) any such consent is given subject to a condition (lawfully imposed) that the tenant is to enter into an agreement guaranteeing the performance of the covenant by the assignee; and

(c) the agreement is entered into by the tenant in pursuance of that condition.

(4) An agreement is not an authorised guarantee agreement to the extent that it purports—

(a) to impose on the tenant any requirement to guarantee in any way the performance of the relevant covenant by any person other than the assignee; or

(b) to impose on the tenant any liability, restriction or other requirement (of whatever nature) in relation to any time after the assignee is released from that covenant by virtue of this Act.

(5) Subject to subsection (4), an authorised guarantee agreement may—

(a) impose on the tenant any liability as sole or principal debtor in respect of any obligation owed by the assignee under the relevant covenant;

(b) impose on the tenant liabilities as guarantor in respect of the assignee's performance of that covenant which are no more onerous than those to which he would be subject in the event of his being liable as sole or principal debtor in respect of any obligation owed by the assignee under that covenant;

(c) require the tenant, in the event of the tenancy assigned by him being disclaimed, to enter into a new tenancy of the premises comprised in the assignment—

(i) whose term expires not later than the term of the tenancy assigned by the tenant, and

(ii) whose tenant covenants are no more onerous than those of that tenancy;

(d) make provision incidental or supplementary to any provision made by virtue of any of paragraphs (a) to (c).

(6) Where a person ("the former tenant") is to any extent released from a covenant of a tenancy by virtue of section 11(2) as from an assignment and the assignor under the assignment enters into an authorised guarantee agreement with the landlord with respect to the performance of that covenant by the assignee under the assignment—

(a) the landlord may require the former tenant to enter into an agreement under which he guarantees, on terms corresponding to those of that authorised guarantee agreement, the performance of that covenant by the assignee under the assignment; and

(b) if its provisions conform with subsections (4) and (5), any such agreement shall be an authorised guarantee agreement for the purposes of this section; and

(c) in the application of this section in relation to any such agreement—

(i) subsections (2)(b) and (c) and (3) shall be omitted, and

(ii) any reference to the tenant or to the assignee shall be read as a reference to the former tenant or to the assignee under the assignment.

(7) For the purposes of subsection (1) it is immaterial that—

> (a) the tenant has already made an authorised guarantee agreement in respect of a previous assignment by him of the tenancy referred to in that subsection, it having been subsequently revested in him following a disclaimer on behalf of the previous assignee, or
>
> (b) the tenancy referred to in that subsection is a new tenancy entered into by the tenant in pursuance of an authorised guarantee agreement;

and in any such case subsections (2) to (5) shall apply accordingly.

(8) It is hereby declared that the rules of law relating to guarantees (and in particular those relating to the release of sureties) are, subject to its terms, applicable in relation to any authorised guarantee agreement as in relation to any other guarantee agreement.

Restriction on liability of former tenant or his guarantor for rent or service charge etc.

17.—(1) This section applies where a person ("the former tenant") is as a result of an assignment no longer a tenant under a tenancy but—

> (a) (in the case of a tenancy which is a new tenancy) he has under an authorised guarantee agreement guaranteed the performance by his assignee of a tenant covenant of the tenancy under which any fixed charge is payable; or
>
> (b) (in the case of any tenancy) he remains bound by such a covenant.

(2) The former tenant shall not be liable under that agreement or (as the case may be) the covenant to pay any amount in respect of any fixed charge payable under the covenant unless, within the period of six months beginning with the date when the charge becomes due, the landlord serves on the former tenant a notice informing him—

> (a) that the charge is now due; and
>
> (b) that in respect of the charge the landlord intends to recover from the former tenant such amount as is specified in the notice and (where payable) interest calculated on such basis as is so specified.

(3) Where a person ("the guarantor") has agreed to guarantee the performance by the former tenant of such a covenant as is mentioned in subsection (1), the guarantor shall not be liable under the agreement to pay any amount in respect of any fixed charge payable under the covenant unless, within the period of six months beginning with the date when the charge becomes due, the landlord serves on the guarantor a notice informing him—

> (a) that the charge is now due; and
>
> (b) that in respect of the charge the landlord intends to recover from the guarantor such amount as is specified in the notice and (where payable) interest calculated on such basis as is so specified.

(4) Where the landlord has duly served a notice under subsection (2) or (3), the amount (exclusive of interest) which the former tenant or (as the case may be) the guarantor is liable to pay in respect of the fixed charge in question shall not exceed the amount specified in the notice unless—

> (a) his liability in respect of the charge is subsequently determined to be for a greater amount,

(b) the notice informed him of the possibility that that liability would be so determined, and

(c) within the period of three months beginning with the date of the determination, the landlord serves on him a further notice informing him that the landlord intends to recover that greater amount from him (plus interest, where payable).

(5) For the purposes of subsection (2) or (3) any fixed charge which has become due before the date on which this Act comes into force shall be treated as becoming due on that date; but neither of those subsections applies to any such charge if before that date proceedings have been instituted by the landlord for the recovery from the former tenant of any amount in respect of it.

(6) In this section—

"fixed charge", in relation to a tenancy, means—

(a) rent,

(b) any service charge as defined by section 18 of the Landlord and Tenant Act 1985 (the words "of a dwelling" being disregarded for this purpose), and   1985 c. 70.

(c) any amount payable under a tenant covenant of the tenancy providing for the payment of a liquidated sum in the event of a failure to comply with any such covenant;

"landlord", in relation to a fixed charge, includes any person who has a right to enforce payment of the charge.

18.—(1) This section applies where a person ("the former tenant") is as a result of an assignment no longer a tenant under a tenancy but—

(a) (in the case of a new tenancy) he has under an authorised guarantee agreement guaranteed the performance by his assignee of any tenant covenant of the tenancy; or

(b) (in the case of any tenancy) he remains bound by such a covenant.

Restriction of liability of former tenant or his guarantor where tenancy subsequently varied.

(2) The former tenant shall not be liable under the agreement or (as the case may be) the covenant to pay any amount in respect of the covenant to the extent that the amount is referable to any relevant variation of the tenant covenants of the tenancy effected after the assignment.

(3) Where a person ("the guarantor") has agreed to guarantee the performance by the former tenant of a tenant covenant of the tenancy, the guarantor (where his liability to do so is not wholly discharged by any such variation of the tenant covenants of the tenancy) shall not be liable under the agreement to pay any amount in respect of the covenant to the extent that the amount is referable to any such variation.

(4) For the purposes of this section a variation of the tenant covenants of a tenancy is a "relevant variation" if either—

(a) the landlord has, at the time of the variation, an absolute right to refuse to allow it; or

(b) the landlord would have had such a right if the variation had been sought by the former tenant immediately before the assignment by him but, between the time of that assignment and the time of the variation, the tenant covenants of the tenancy have been so varied as to deprive the landlord of such a right.

(5) In determining whether the landlord has or would have had such a right at any particular time regard shall be had to all the circumstances (including the effect of any provision made by or under any enactment).

(6) Nothing in this section applies to any variation of the tenant covenants of a tenancy effected before the date on which this Act comes into force.

(7) In this section "variation" means a variation whether effected by deed or otherwise.

Overriding leases

Right of former tenant or his guarantor to overriding lease.

19.—(1) Where in respect of any tenancy ("the relevant tenancy") any person ("the claimant") makes full payment of an amount which he has been duly required to pay in accordance with section 17, together with any interest payable, he shall be entitled (subject to and in accordance with this section) to have the landlord under that tenancy grant him an overriding lease of the premises demised by the tenancy.

(2) For the purposes of this section "overriding lease" means a tenancy of the reversion expectant on the relevant tenancy which—

    (a) is granted for a term equal to the remainder of the term of the relevant tenancy plus three days or the longest period (less than three days) that will not wholly displace the landlord's reversionary interest expectant on the relevant tenancy, as the case may require; and

    (b) (subject to subsections (3) and (4) and to any modifications agreed to by the claimant and the landlord) otherwise contains the same covenants as the relevant tenancy, as they have effect immediately before the grant of the lease.

(3) An overriding lease shall not be required to reproduce any covenant of the relevant tenancy to the extent that the covenant is (in whatever terms) expressed to be a personal covenant between the landlord and the tenant under that tenancy.

(4) If any right, liability or other matter arising under a covenant of the relevant tenancy falls to be determined or otherwise operates (whether expressly or otherwise) by reference to the commencement of that tenancy—

    (a) the corresponding covenant of the overriding lease shall be so framed that that right, liability or matter falls to be determined or otherwise operates by reference to the commencement of that tenancy; but

    (b) the overriding lease shall not be required to reproduce any covenant of that tenancy to the extent that it has become spent by the time that that lease is granted.

(5) A claim to exercise the right to an overriding lease under this section is made by the claimant making a request for such a lease to the landlord; and any such request—

    (a) must be made to the landlord in writing and specify the payment by virtue of which the claimant claims to be entitled to the lease ("the qualifying payment"); and

(b) must be so made at the time of making the qualifying payment or within the period of 12 months beginning with the date of that payment.

(6) Where the claimant duly makes such a request—

(a) the landlord shall (subject to subsection (7)) grant and deliver to the claimant an overriding lease of the demised premises within a reasonable time of the request being received by the landlord; and

(b) the claimant—

(i) shall thereupon deliver to the landlord a counterpart of the lease duly executed by the claimant, and

(ii) shall be liable for the landlord's reasonable costs of and incidental to the grant of the lease.

(7) The landlord shall not be under any obligation to grant an overriding lease of the demised premises under this section at a time when the relevant tenancy has been determined; and a claimant shall not be entitled to the grant of such a lease if at the time when he makes his request—

(a) the landlord has already granted such a lease and that lease remains in force; or

(b) another person has already duly made a request for such a lease to the landlord and that request has been neither withdrawn nor abandoned by that person.

(8) Where two or more requests are duly made on the same day, then for the purposes of subsection (7)—

(a) a request made by a person who was liable for the qualifying payment as a former tenant shall be treated as made before a request made by a person who was so liable as a guarantor; and

(b) a request made by a person whose liability in respect of the covenant in question commenced earlier than any such liability of another person shall be treated as made before a request made by that other person.

(9) Where a claimant who has duly made a request for an overriding lease under this section subsequently withdraws or abandons the request before he is granted such a lease by the landlord, the claimant shall be liable for the landlord's reasonable costs incurred in pursuance of the request down to the time of its withdrawal or abandonment; and for the purposes of this section—

(a) a claimant's request is withdrawn by the claimant notifying the landlord in writing that he is withdrawing his request; and

(b) a claimant is to be regarded as having abandoned his request if—

(i) the landlord has requested the claimant in writing to take, within such reasonable period as is specified in the landlord's request, all or any of the remaining steps required to be taken by the claimant before the lease can be granted, and

(ii) the claimant fails to comply with the landlord's request,

and is accordingly to be regarded as having abandoned it at the time when that period expires.

(10) Any request or notification under this section may be sent by post.

(11) The preceding provisions of this section shall apply where the landlord is the tenant under an overriding lease granted under this section as they apply where no such lease has been granted; and accordingly there may be two or more such leases interposed between the first such lease and the relevant tenancy.

Overriding leases: supplementary provisions.

20.—(1) For the purposes of section 1 an overriding lease shall be a new tenancy only if the relevant tenancy is a new tenancy.

(2) Every overriding lease shall state—

    (a) that it is a lease granted under section 19, and

    (b) whether it is or is not a new tenancy for the purposes of section 1;

1925 c. 21.

and any such statement shall comply with such requirements as may be prescribed by rules made in pursuance of section 144 of the Land Registration Act 1925 (power to make general rules).

(3) A claim that the landlord has failed to comply with subsection (6)(a) of section 19 may be made the subject of civil proceedings in like manner as any other claim in tort for breach of statutory duty; and if the claimant under that section fails to comply with subsection (6)(b)(i) of that section he shall not be entitled to exercise any of the rights otherwise exercisable by him under the overriding lease.

(4) An overriding lease—

    (a) shall be deemed to be authorised as against the persons interested in any mortgage of the landlord's interest (however created or arising); and

    (b) shall be binding on any such persons;

and if any such person is by virtue of such a mortgage entitled to possession of the documents of title relating to the landlord's interest—

    (i) the landlord shall within one month of the execution of the lease deliver to that person the counterpart executed in pursuance of section 19(6)(b)(i); and

    (ii) if he fails to do so, the instrument creating or evidencing the mortgage shall apply as if the obligation to deliver a counterpart were included in the terms of the mortgage as set out in that instrument.

(5) It is hereby declared—

    (a) that the fact that an overriding lease takes effect subject to the relevant tenancy shall not constitute a breach of any covenant of the lease against subletting or parting with possession of the premises demised by the lease or any part of them; and

    (b) that each of sections 16, 17 and 18 applies where the tenancy referred to in subsection (1) of that section is an overriding lease as it applies in other cases falling within that subsection.

1972 c. 61.

(6) No tenancy shall be registrable under the Land Charges Act 1972 or be taken to be an estate contract within the meaning of that Act by reason of any right or obligation that may arise under section 19, and any right arising from a request made under that section shall not be an overriding interest within the meaning of the Land Registration Act 1925;

but any such request shall be registrable under the Land Charges Act 1972, or may be the subject of a notice or caution under the Land Registration Act 1925, as if it were an estate contract.

1972 c. 61.
1925 c. 21.

(7) In this section—

(a) "mortgage" includes "charge"; and

(b) any expression which is also used in section 19 has the same meaning as in that section.

Forfeiture and disclaimer

21.—(1) Where—

(a) as a result of one or more assignments a person is the tenant of part only of the premises demised by a tenancy, and

(b) under a proviso or stipulation in the tenancy there is a right of re-entry or forfeiture for a breach of a tenant covenant of the tenancy, and

(c) the right is (apart from this subsection) exercisable in relation to that part and other land demised by the tenancy,

the right shall nevertheless, in connection with a breach of any such covenant by that person, be taken to be a right exercisable only in relation to that part.

Forfeiture or disclaimer limited to part only of demised premises.

(2) Where—

(a) a company which is being wound up, or a trustee in bankruptcy, is as a result of one or more assignments the tenant of part only of the premises demised by a tenancy, and

(b) the liquidator of the company exercises his power under section 178 of the Insolvency Act 1986, or the trustee in bankruptcy exercises his power under section 315 of that Act, to disclaim property demised by the tenancy,

the power is exercisable only in relation to the part of the premises referred to in paragraph (a).

1986 c. 45.

Landlord's consent to assignments

22. After subsection (1) of section 19 of the Landlord and Tenant Act 1927 (provisions as to covenants not to assign etc. without licence or consent) there shall be inserted—

Imposition of conditions regulating giving of landlord's consent to assignments.
1927 c. 36.

"(1A) Where the landlord and the tenant under a qualifying lease have entered into an agreement specifying for the purposes of this subsection—

(a) any circumstances in which the landlord may withhold his licence or consent to an assignment of the demised premises or any part of them, or

(b) any conditions subject to which any such licence or consent may be granted,

then the landlord—

(i) shall not be regarded as unreasonably withholding his licence or consent to any such assignment if he withholds it on the ground (and it is the case) that any such circumstances exist, and

95

> (ii) if he gives any such licence or consent subject to any such conditions, shall not be regarded as giving it subject to unreasonable conditions;

and section 1 of the Landlord and Tenant Act 1988 (qualified duty to consent to assignment etc.) shall have effect subject to the provisions of this subsection.

(1B) Subsection (1A) of this section applies to such an agreement as is mentioned in that subsection—

> (a) whether it is contained in the lease or not, and
>
> (b) whether it is made at the time when the lease is granted or at any other time falling before the application for the landlord's licence or consent is made.

(1C) Subsection (1A) shall not, however, apply to any such agreement to the extent that any circumstances or conditions specified in it are framed by reference to any matter falling to be determined by the landlord or by any other person for the purposes of the agreement, unless under the terms of the agreement—

> (a) that person's power to determine that matter is required to be exercised reasonably, or
>
> (b) the tenant is given an unrestricted right to have any such determination reviewed by a person independent of both landlord and tenant whose identity is ascertainable by reference to the agreement,

and in the latter case the agreement provides for the determination made by any such independent person on the review to be conclusive as to the matter in question.

(1D) In its application to a qualifying lease, subsection (1)(b) of this section shall not have effect in relation to any assignment of the lease.

(1E) In subsections (1A) and (1D) of this section—

> (a) "qualifying lease" means any lease which is a new tenancy for the purposes of section 1 of the Landlord and Tenant (Covenants) Act 1995 other than a residential lease, namely a lease by which a building or part of a building is let wholly or mainly as a single private residence; and
>
> (b) references to assignment include parting with possession on assignment."

Supplemental

Effects of becoming subject to liability under, or entitled to benefit of, covenant etc.

23.—(1) Where as a result of an assignment a person becomes, by virtue of this Act, bound by or entitled to the benefit of a covenant, he shall not by virtue of this Act have any liability or rights under the covenant in relation to any time falling before the assignment.

(2) Subsection (1) does not preclude any such rights being expressly assigned to the person in question.

(3) Where as a result of an assignment a person becomes, by virtue of this Act, entitled to a right of re-entry contained in a tenancy, that right shall be exercisable in relation to any breach of a covenant of the tenancy

occurring before the assignment as in relation to one occurring thereafter, unless by reason of any waiver or release it was not so exercisable immediately before the assignment.

24.—(1) Any release of a person from a covenant by virtue of this Act does not affect any liability of his arising from a breach of the covenant occurring before the release.

(2) Where—

   (a) by virtue of this Act a tenant is released from a tenant covenant of a tenancy, and

   (b) immediately before the release another person is bound by a covenant of the tenancy imposing any liability or penalty in the event of a failure to comply with that tenant covenant,

then, as from the release of the tenant, that other person is released from the covenant mentioned in paragraph (b) to the same extent as the tenant is released from that tenant covenant.

(3) Where a person bound by a landlord or tenant covenant of a tenancy—

   (a) assigns the whole or part of his interest in the premises demised by the tenancy, but

   (b) is not released by virtue of this Act from the covenant (with the result that subsection (1) does not apply),

the assignment does not affect any liability of his arising from a breach of the covenant occurring before the assignment.

(4) Where by virtue of this Act a person ceases to be entitled to the benefit of a covenant, this does not affect any rights of his arising from a breach of the covenant occurring before he ceases to be so entitled.

Effects of release from liability under, or loss of benefit of, covenant.

25.—(1) Any agreement relating to a tenancy is void to the extent that—

   (a) it would apart from this section have effect to exclude, modify or otherwise frustrate the operation of any provision of this Act, or

   (b) it provides for—

      (i) the termination or surrender of the tenancy, or

      (ii) the imposition on the tenant of any penalty, disability or liability,

   in the event of the operation of any provision of this Act, or

   (c) it provides for any of the matters referred to in paragraph (b)(i) or (ii) and does so (whether expressly or otherwise) in connection with, or in consequence of, the operation of any provision of this Act.

(2) To the extent that an agreement relating to a tenancy constitutes a covenant (whether absolute or qualified) against the assignment, or parting with the possession, of the premises demised by the tenancy or any part of them—

   (a) the agreement is not void by virtue of subsection (1) by reason only of the fact that as such the covenant prohibits or restricts any such assignment or parting with possession; but

Agreement void if it restricts operation of the Act.

(b) paragraph (a) above does not otherwise affect the operation of that subsection in relation to the agreement (and in particular does not preclude its application to the agreement to the extent that it purports to regulate the giving of, or the making of any application for, consent to any such assignment or parting with possession).

(3) In accordance with section 16(1) nothing in this section applies to any agreement to the extent that it is an authorised guarantee agreement; but (without prejudice to the generality of subsection (1) above) an agreement is void to the extent that it is one falling within section 16(4)(a) or (b).

(4) This section applies to an agreement relating to a tenancy whether or not the agreement is—

(a) contained in the instrument creating the tenancy; or

(b) made before the creation of the tenancy.

Miscellaneous savings etc.

26.—(1) Nothing in this Act is to be read as preventing—

(a) a party to a tenancy from releasing a person from a landlord covenant or a tenant covenant of the tenancy; or

(b) the parties to a tenancy from agreeing to an apportionment of liability under such a covenant.

1985 c. 70.

(2) Nothing in this Act affects the operation of section 3(3A) of the Landlord and Tenant Act 1985 (preservation of former landlord's liability until tenant notified of new landlord).

(3) No apportionment which has become binding in accordance with section 10 shall be affected by any order or decision made under or by virtue of any enactment not contained in this Act which relates to apportionment.

Notices for the purposes of the Act.

27.—(1) The form of any notice to be served for the purposes of section 8, 10 or 17 shall be prescribed by regulations made by the Lord Chancellor by statutory instrument.

(2) The regulations shall require any notice served for the purposes of section 8(1) or 10(1) ("the initial notice") to include—

(a) an explanation of the significance of the notice and the options available to the person on whom it is served;

(b) a statement that any objections to the proposed release, or (as the case may be) to the proposed binding effect of the apportionment, must be made by notice in writing served on the person or persons by whom the initial notice is served within the period of four weeks beginning with the day on which the initial notice is served; and

(c) an address in England and Wales to which any such objections may be sent.

(3) The regulations shall require any notice served for the purposes of section 17 to include an explanation of the significance of the notice.

(4) If any notice purporting to be served for the purposes of section 8(1), 10(1) or 17 is not in the prescribed form, or in a form substantially to the same effect, the notice shall not be effective for the purposes of section 8, section 10 or section 17 (as the case may be).

(5) Section 23 of the Landlord and Tenant Act 1927 shall apply in relation to the service of notices for the purposes of section 8, 10 or 17. 1927 c. 36.

(6) Any statutory instrument made under this section shall be subject to annulment in pursuance of a resolution of either House of Parliament.

28.—(1) In this Act (unless the context otherwise requires)— Interpretation.

"assignment" includes equitable assignment and in addition (subject to section 11) assignment in breach of a covenant of a tenancy or by operation of law;

"authorised guarantee agreement" means an agreement which is an authorised guarantee agreement for the purposes of section 16;

"collateral agreement", in relation to a tenancy, means any agreement collateral to the tenancy, whether made before or after its creation;

"consent" includes licence;

"covenant" includes term, condition and obligation, and references to a covenant (or any description of covenant) of a tenancy include a covenant (or a covenant of that description) contained in a collateral agreement;

"landlord" and "tenant", in relation to a tenancy, mean the person for the time being entitled to the reversion expectant on the term of the tenancy and the person so entitled to that term respectively;

"landlord covenant", in relation to a tenancy, means a covenant falling to be complied with by the landlord of premises demised by the tenancy;

"new tenancy" means a tenancy which is a new tenancy for the purposes of section 1;

"reversion" means the interest expectant on the termination of a tenancy;

"tenancy" means any lease or other tenancy and includes—

(a) a sub-tenancy, and

(b) an agreement for a tenancy,

but does not include a mortgage term;

"tenant covenant", in relation to a tenancy, means a covenant falling to be complied with by the tenant of premises demised by the tenancy.

(2) For the purposes of any reference in this Act to a covenant falling to be complied with in relation to a particular part of the premises demised by a tenancy, a covenant falls to be so complied with if—

(a) it in terms applies to that part of the premises, or

(b) in its practical application it can be attributed to that part of the premises (whether or not it can also be so attributed to other individual parts of those premises).

(3) Subsection (2) does not apply in relation to covenants to pay money; and, for the purposes of any reference in this Act to a covenant falling to be complied with in relation to a particular part of the premises demised by a tenancy, a covenant of a tenancy which is a covenant to pay money falls to be so complied with if—

(a) the covenant in terms applies to that part; or

(b) the amount of the payment is determinable specifically by reference—

(i) to that part, or

(ii) to anything falling to be done by or for a person as tenant or occupier of that part (if it is a tenant covenant), or

(iii) to anything falling to be done by or for a person as landlord of that part (if it is a landlord covenant).

(4) Where two or more persons jointly constitute either the landlord or the tenant in relation to a tenancy, any reference in this Act to the landlord or the tenant is a reference to both or all of the persons who jointly constitute the landlord or the tenant, as the case may be (and accordingly nothing in section 13 applies in relation to the rights and liabilities of such persons between themselves).

(5) References in this Act to the assignment by a landlord of the reversion in the whole or part of the premises demised by a tenancy are to the assignment by him of the whole of his interest (as owner of the reversion) in the whole or part of those premises.

(6) For the purposes of this Act—

(a) any assignment (however effected) consisting in the transfer of the whole of the landlord's interest (as owner of the reversion) in any premises demised by a tenancy shall be treated as an assignment by the landlord of the reversion in those premises even if it is not effected by him; and

(b) any assignment (however effected) consisting in the transfer of the whole of the tenant's interest in any premises demised by a tenancy shall be treated as an assignment by the tenant of those premises even if it is not effected by him.

Crown application.

29. This Act binds the Crown.

Consequential amendments and repeals.

30.—(1) The enactments specified in Schedule 1 are amended in accordance with that Schedule, the amendments being consequential on the provisions of this Act.

(2) The enactments specified in Schedule 2 are repealed to the extent specified.

(3) Subsections (1) and (2) do not affect the operation of—

1925 c. 20.

(a) section 77 of, or Part IX or X of Schedule 2 to, the Law of Property Act 1925, or

1925 c. 21.

(b) section 24(1)(b) or (2) of the Land Registration Act 1925,

in relation to tenancies which are not new tenancies.

(4) In consequence of this Act nothing in the following provisions, namely—

(a) sections 78 and 79 of the Law of Property Act 1925 (benefit and burden of covenants relating to land), and

(b) sections 141 and 142 of that Act (running of benefit and burden of covenants with reversion),

shall apply in relation to new tenancies.

(5) The Lord Chancellor may by order made by statutory instrument make, in the case of such enactments as may be specified in the order, such amendments or repeals in, or such modifications of, those enactments as appear to him to be necessary or expedient in consequence of any provision of this Act.

(6) Any statutory instrument made under subsection (5) shall be subject to annulment in pursuance of a resolution of either House of Parliament.

31.—(1) The provisions of this Act come into force on such day as the Lord Chancellor may appoint by order made by statutory instrument.

Commencement.

(2) An order under this section may contain such transitional provisions and savings (whether or not involving the modification of any enactment) as appear to the Lord Chancellor necessary or expedient in connection with the provisions brought into force by the order.

32.—(1) This Act may be cited as the Landlord and Tenant (Covenants) Act 1995.

Short title and extent.

(2) This Act extends to England and Wales only.

SCHEDULES

SCHEDULE 1

CONSEQUENTIAL AMENDMENTS

Trustee Act 1925 (c.19)

1. In section 26 of the Trustee Act 1925 (protection against liability in respect of rents and covenants), after subsection (1) insert—

> "(1A) Where a personal representative or trustee has as such entered into, or may as such be required to enter into, an authorised guarantee agreement with respect to any lease comprised in the estate of a deceased testator or intestate or a trust estate (and, in a case where he has entered into such an agreement, he has satisfied all liabilities under it which may have accrued and been claimed up to the date of distribution)—
>
> > (a) he may distribute the residuary real and personal estate of the deceased testator or intestate, or the trust estate, to or amongst the persons entitled thereto—
> >
> > > (i) without appropriating any part of the estate of the deceased, or the trust estate, to meet any future liability (or, as the case may be, any liability) under any such agreement, and
> > >
> > > (ii) notwithstanding any potential liability of his to enter into any such agreement; and
> >
> > (b) notwithstanding such distribution, he shall not be personally liable in respect of any subsequent claim (or, as the case may be, any claim) under any such agreement.
>
> In this subsection "authorised guarantee agreement" has the same meaning as in the Landlord and Tenant (Covenants) Act 1995."

Law of Property Act 1925 (c.20)

2. In section 77 of the Law of Property Act 1925 (implied covenants in conveyances subject to rents), for subsection (2) substitute—

> "(2) Where in a conveyance for valuable consideration, other than a mortgage, part of land affected by a rentcharge is, without the consent of the owner of the rentcharge, expressed to be conveyed subject to or charged with the entire rent, paragraph (B)(i) of subsection (1) of this section shall apply as if, in paragraph (i) of Part VIII of the Second Schedule to this Act—
>
> > (a) any reference to the apportioned rent were to the entire rent; and
> >
> > (b) the words "(other than the covenant to pay the entire rent)" were omitted.
>
> (2A) Where in a conveyance for valuable consideration, other than a mortgage, part of land affected by a rentcharge is, without the consent of the owner of the rentcharge, expressed to be conveyed discharged or exonerated from the entire rent, paragraph (B)(ii) of subsection (1) of this section shall apply as if, in paragraph (ii) of Part VIII of the Second Schedule to this Act—
>
> > (a) any reference to the balance of the rent were to the entire rent; and
> >
> > (b) the words ", other than the covenant to pay the entire rent," were omitted."

Landlord and Tenant Act 1954 (c.56)

3. At the end of section 34 of the Landlord and Tenant Act 1954 (rent under new tenancy) insert—

"(4) It is hereby declared that the matters which are to be taken into account by the court in determining the rent include any effect on rent of the operation of the provisions of the Landlord and Tenant (Covenants) Act 1995."

4.—(1) The existing provisions of section 35 of that Act (other terms of new tenancy) shall constitute subsection (1) of that section.

(2) After those provisions insert—

"(2) In subsection (1) of this section the reference to all relevant circumstances includes (without prejudice to the generality of that reference) a reference to the operation of the provisions of the Landlord and Tenant (Covenants) Act 1995."

SCHEDULE 2

Section 30(2).

REPEALS

Chapter	Short title	Extent of repeal
15 & 16 Geo.5 c.20.	Law of Property Act 1925.	In section 77, subsection (1)(C) and (D) and, in subsection (7), paragraph (c) and the "or" preceding it. In Schedule 2, Parts IX and X.
15 & 16 Geo.5 c.21.	Land Registration Act 1925.	Section 24(1)(b) and (2).

precedents

NB: Terms in *italics* in these draft clauses are assumed to have been defined elsewhere in the lease.

Precedent 1: Applying the new regime to a lease granted before the commencement date

NEW CLAUSE[1]

This *Lease* shall be construed as if:

A.1   sections 5, 11(1), (2) and (7), 13(1) and (2), 24 and 28(1) and (4) of the Landlord and Tenant (Covenants) Act 1995[2] were in force at the date of grant of this *Lease* and

A.2   this *Lease* was a new tenancy as defined by that Act.

NEW ASSIGNMENT PROVISION[3]

B.1   Not to assign the whole of the *Demised Premises* save in the circumstances mentioned in B.2.

B.2   Not to assign the whole of the *Demised Premises* without first applying to the *Landlord* for consent to assign and at the time of making that application complying with the conditions set out in clause B.3 and:—

B.2.1 obtaining the written consent of the *Landlord* which shall not be unreasonably withheld; and

B2.2 procuring that, upon or before any assignment and before giving occupation to the assignee, if the *Landlord* shall reasonably so require, the assignee shall obtain guarantors reasonably acceptable to the *Landlord* who shall covenant by way of indemnity and guarantee (if more than one jointly and severally) with the *Landlord* before any assignment in the terms set out in Schedule [contractual guarantee[4]] of this *Lease*.

B.3 The conditions referred to in clause B.2 are that:—

B.3.1 the *Tenant* shall obtain and deliver to the *Landlord* a direct covenant by the assignee with the *Landlord* to observe and perform the tenant covenants of this *Lease* and any deed, licence, consent or other instrument supplemental to this *Lease* during any period when by virtue of the Landlord and Tenant (Covenants) Act 1995 (as applied to this *Lease* by clause A) the assignee is bound by the tenant covenants of this *Lease*;[5] and

[B.3.2 the *Tenant* shall deliver to the *Landlord* a covenant by way of indemnity and guarantee with the *Landlord* in the terms set out in Schedule [authorised guarantee agreement][6]].

RENT REVIEW[7]

The hypothetical lease should be deemed to be construed as if it were a lease other than a new lease for the purposes of section 1 of the 1995 Act.

LANDLORD'S COVENANT[8]

C.5 The *Landlord* covenants with the *Tenant* not to transfer its estate and interest in the *Demised Premises* without first obtaining and delivering to the *Tenant* a direct covenant by the transferee with the *Tenant* to observe and perform the landlord covenants and restrictions of this *Lease* (including this sub-clause) and any deed, licence, consent or other instrument supplemental to this *Lease* for the remainder of the *Term*.

1. The general objective of this precedent is to create for the landlord and tenant a regime of covenants which, while applying in so far as possible the new privity regime to an old lease, would not cause problems of enforcement for either party under the existing law.

Certain provisions of the new regime cannot be incorporated by reference into a lease granted before the 1995 Act comes into force. The provisions concerned are those which before the commencement date of that Act are already governed by a statute from which there can be no contracting out, e.g. section 19(1)(a) of the 1927 Act. However, to the extent that the 1995 Act contains provisions (such as release from original tenant liability) which could have been grafted onto leases in the past by agreement, then it may be incorporated before the Act comes into force.

Unless otherwise indicated, these amendments are broadly neutral and could be used by either a landlord or a tenant where it has been agreed to apply the new law to a lease being granted before it comes into force.

They are simple provisions which do not deal with the various notices under the Act which have to be in prescribed forms. The notice provisions could only be incorporated by drafting which is disproportionately complex in relation to what is being sought. However, if there is a delay in bringing the Act into force, consider providing contractual equivalents of those notices. If it is known that the Act is to be brought into force shortly, it may be considered unlikely that any need to serve the various notices will arise in the interim.

2. It is not possible to apply by private contract the new provisions about the way in which leasehold covenants run.

3. It is not possible to apply the new section 19(1A) of the 1927 Act until the 1995 Act actually comes into force—hence the provisions introduce a regime of covenants which, from the landlord's perspective, are appropriate to the new regime required by the tenant, while adopting a structure which has been successfully tested in the landlord's favour under the 1927 Act. The particular point to note is that the clause contains enforceable conditions precedent (see *Bocardo v S and M Hotels Ltd* [1980] 1 WLR 17). If a landlord is prepared to allow the tenant to have the benefit of the release provisions of the new lease but desires to control the operation of the release then the way forward is not to allow the incorporation by reference to the Act but instead to introduce into the alienation clause a pre-condition to licence to assign that the assignee meets certain criteria. However, there must be some doubt whether a *Bocardo*-style clause inserted in an existing lease purporting to set pre-conditions for assignment by defining an acceptable assignee would be upheld. It would be less risky for the clause simply to separate the issue of who is an acceptable assignee from the issue of whether the assignor can be released from liability. The cautious approach, therefore, is simply to set out tests (by reference usually to the financial strength of the assignee) for the release from liability of the assignor.

4. Landlords will want the contractual guarantee to be expressed to cover the assignee's liability while he is bound by the tenant covenants of the lease (see footnote 6).

5. The direct covenant to make all the tenant's covenants run is necessary because of the point mentioned in note 1 and the exclusion of the sections of the Act dealing with the transmission of covenants.

6. Tenants may not want to offer B.3.2. See chapter 3 of the text for information about the contents of an AGA. Landlords will want to express the authorised guarantor's liability to last while the assignee is bound by the tenant covenants of the lease, rather than while the lease is vested in the assignee, to cover the possibility of an excluded assignment by the assignee.

7. Rent review clauses are drafted in many styles. This describes the effect to be achieved by amending the clause, rather than suggesting specific wording.

8. This clause is necessary to create continuing liability for successor landlords on which the release under the Act can bite. Landlords may not wish to include it.

Precedent 2: Sample assignment conditions in a new lease

D.1 Not to assign the whole of the *Demised Premises* without first:—

D.1.1 obtaining the written licence of the *Landlord* which shall not be unreasonably withheld;

D.1.2 satisfying the circumstances specified for the purposes of section 19(1A)[1] of the Landlord and Tenant Act 1927 and set out in clause D.2.1 below; and

D.1.3 complying with the conditions specified for the purposes of section 19(1A)[1] of the Landlord and Tenant Act 1927 and set out in clause D.2.2 below.

D.2.1 The circumstances[2] referred to in clause D.1.2 are that:—

D.2.1.1 all sums due from the *Tenant* under this *Lease* have been paid at the date of the application for the licence to assign;

D.2.1.2 in the *Landlord's* reasonable opinion there are at the date of the application for the licence to assign no material outstanding breaches of any tenant covenant under this *Lease* or any personal covenants undertaken by the *Tenant*;

D.2.1.3 in the *Landlord's* reasonable opinion the assignee is a person who is at the date of the application for licence to assign no less likely than the *Tenant* was at the date on which this *Lease* was assigned or granted to the *Tenant* to be able to comply with the tenant covenants of this *Lease* and is likely to continue to be such a person following the assignment; and

D.2.1.4 the assignee is a Qualifying Person.

D.2.2 The conditions[2] referred to in clause D.1.3 are that:—

D.2.2.1 upon or before any assignment and before giving occupation to the assignee the *Tenant* shall covenant by way of indemnity and guarantee with the *Landlord* in the terms set out in Schedule [authorised guarantee agreement[3]];

D.2.2.2 if so reasonably required by the *Landlord* the assignee shall upon or before any assignment and before taking occupation obtain guarantors reasonably acceptable to the *Landlord* who shall covenant by way of indemnity and guarantee (if more than one jointly and severally) with the *Landlord* in the terms set out in Schedule [contractual guarantee[4]]; and

D.2.2.3 the written licence to assign contains a condition that if at any time prior to the assignment the circumstances (or any of them) specified in clause D.2.1 cease to exist the *Landlord* may revoke the licence by written notice to the *Tenant*.

D.3 'Qualifying Person' means an assignee who:—

FACTUAL TEST

D.3.1 is a public limited company incorporated in England and Wales with:—

D.3.1.1 annual profits before tax in the [three] complete trading years immediately preceding the date of the application for licence to assign which in each year [and after consolidation (whether real or notional) in each such year with the annual profits before tax of any subsidiary within the meaning of section 736 of the Companies Act 1985)] exceed an amount representing the yearly rent payable under the *Lease* at the date of that application multiplied by [three] as evidenced by a set of properly audited accounts [the latest set of which was published not earlier than [eleven] months before the date of the application]; or

D.3.1.2 net assets (from which there is excluded any amount in deferred tax) which at the date of the application for licence to assign [and after consolidation (whether real or notional) with the net assets (from which there is excluded any amount in deferred tax) of any subsidiary (within the meaning of section 736 of the Companies Act 1985)] exceed an amount representing the yearly rent payable under the *Lease* at the date of that application multiplied by [three] as evidenced by a set of properly audited accounts [the latest set of which was published not earlier than [eleven] months before the date of the application];

REASONABLE DISCRETION TEST

D.3.2 together with any guarantees and other security for the performance by the assignee of the tenant covenants under this *Lease* (other than any authorised guarantee agreement as described in section 16 of the Landlord and Tenant (Covenants) Act 1995) is in the reasonable opinion of the *Landlord* no less substantial in financial terms than the *Tenant* and the *Guarantor*[5] were [are] in aggregate at the date on which this *Lease* was assigned or granted[6] to the *Tenant* [at the date of the application for the licence to assign] (after taking into account the value at that date of any other security for the performance of the tenant covenants under this *Lease* by the *Tenant*);

APPEAL FROM LANDLORD'S DISCRETION TO THIRD PARTY

D.3.3 proposes to use the *Demised Premises* for a purpose which, in the *Landlord's* opinion, complies with the *Landlord's* tenant mix policy in force at the date of the application for licence to assign and available for inspection by the *Tenant* on the *Tenant* giving reasonable prior notice in writing, but the *Tenant* may within [14] days of being notified in writing of the *Landlord's* decision give to the *Landlord* written notice requiring the question to be referred to an independent surveyor:—

D.3.3.1 who shall act as an expert [but who shall invite written submissions from the parties] [in accordance with directions he shall make to the parties in writing];

D.3.3.2 whose decision shall be conclusive;

D.3.3.3 who shall be appointed by agreement between the parties or in the absence of agreement [within 14 days] shall be nominated by the President for the time being of the Royal Institution of Chartered Surveyors on the application of either party;

D.3.3.4 whose fees and expenses (including the cost of his appointment) shall be borne equally by the *Landlord* and the *Tenant* who shall otherwise bear their own costs.

NB These clauses are for illustrative purposes only, to show how to draft the various different types of conditions. They are not intended to indicate what would be appropriate in any particular case. Nor are they to be taken as suggesting, for example, that a specific profits test is preferable to no test, or a more general test (e.g. simply requiring the assignee to demonstrate that it can, and will be likely to continue to be able, to honour the tenant covenants).

1. The draftsman should adopt a cautious construction of section 19(1A) of the 1927 Act (inserted by the 1995 Act) which requires the alienation clause to state that the conditions and circumstances which it mentions are specified for the purposes of that sub-section.

2. The Act distinguishes between specifying 'circumstances' on the one hand and 'conditions' on the other. The 'circumstances' are those in which the landlord may withhold his licence. This indicates that the landlord is to check the existence of the circumstances when deciding whether to give the licence. 'Conditions' are expressed to be matters 'subject to which any such licence . . . may be granted'. This suggests that what is being anticipated is a licence which states that the assignment cannot take place until certain conditions are satisfied. The conditions are conditions precedent to the assignment. Clauses D.1 and D.2 are drafted on this assumption and seek clearly to distinguish between 'circumstances' and 'conditions'. There will be circumstances which the landlord requires to exist before, and to continue to exist after, the licence to assign has been given up to the date of the assignment (when the die is cast and the lease covenants bind the assignee).

3. See chapter 3 of the text for information about the contents of an AGA. Landlords will want to express the authorised guarantor's liability to last while the assignee is bound by the tenant covenants of the lease, rather than while the lease is vested in the assignee, to cover the possibility of an excluded assignment by the assignee.

4. Landlords will want the contractual guarantee to be expressed to cover the assignee's liability while he is bound by the tenant covenants of the lease (see footnote 3) and any period during which the assignee is liable under an AGA—see chapter 3 of the text.

5. In other words the current tenant's contractual guarantor. Where the tenant is worthless but backed by a substantial guarantor it is important that any measure of equivalent financial status takes into account the whole existing package of security, not just the current tenant's financial position.

6. Consider whether the time at which the tenant's financial status is measured should be when he acquired the lease (when his status was acceptable to the landlord) or at the date of the application for licence to assign (when it may have deteriorated sharply). On the other hand, the outgoing tenant may be a better covenant now than when he acquired the lease: the wily landlord may wish to leave himself free to pick whichever of the two dates gives the better picture.

Precedent 3: Extending the tenant's rights under a new lease
E DEFAULT NOTICES

E.1 The *Landlord* covenants that, before attempting to recover any such payment as is described in E.2 from the *Guarantor*, it will serve on the *Guarantor* a notice as if that payment was a fixed charge under the Landlord and Tenant (Covenants) Act 1995.

E.2 The payment referred to in E.1 is any amount payable in respect of any breach of covenant by the *Tenant* which:—

E.2.1 has been finally determined by a court or in binding arbitration; or

E.2.2 has been agreed between the *Landlord* and the *Tenant*.

E.3 The notice in respect of the payments referred to in E.2 shall be in the form prescribed by section 27 of the Landlord and Tenant (Covenants) Act 1995 with such variations as may be appropriate to the circumstances.

E.4 No *Guarantor* will be liable for any of the payments referred to in E.2 unless, within the period of six months of the payment being determined or agreed, the *Landlord* serves on the *Guarantor* a notice under this clause.

Clause E is a tenant's amendment which widens the circumstances in which a default notice must be served. It should be inserted in the authorised guarantee provisions because once a former tenant has been released as tenant he loses the benefit of the landlord covenants in the lease. The authorised guarantee will be entered into afresh on assignment. A tenant safeguarding the interests of his own or future contractual guarantors will also want to insert it in the contractual guarantee.

Precedent 4: Contract clause for assignment of existing lease
F OVERRIDING LEASE

F.1 In this clause F:—

F.1.1 'the Act' means the Landlord and Tenant (Covenants) Act 1995;

F.1.2 'the Overriding Lease' means an overriding lease pursuant to section 19 of the Act;

F.1.3 'the Landlord' means the reversioner from time to time of the *Leas[e*; and

F.1.4 'the Underlease' means an underlease granted pursuant to clause F.5.3].

F.2 This clause applies if:—

F.2.1 the *Seller* makes a payment in respect of the *Lease* pursuant to a notice under section 17 of the Act;

F.2.2 the *Seller* has not claimed an Overriding Lease in consequence of that payment; and

F.2.3 the *Buyer* has fully indemnified the *Seller* in respect of that payment pursuant to clause [indemnity covenant] of this [contract/transfer].

F.3 At the time of making the indemnity payment to the *Seller* or within the period of [six] months beginning with the date of that payment the *Buyer* may by notice in writing request the *Seller* to claim an Overriding Lease.

F.4 The Overriding Lease shall be in such form as may be required by sections 19 and 20 of the Act with such variations as the Landlord and the *Seller* (the latter acting at the direction of and with the consent of the *Buyer*) may agree.[1]

F.5[.1] The *Seller* shall use its reasonable endeavours to obtain the Landlord's licence for the assignment of the Overriding Lease to the *Buyer* but shall not be required to commence proceedings for a declaration that consent is being unreasonably withheld.

[F.5.2 If licence for assignment of the Overriding Lease to the *Buyer* is withheld the *Seller* shall use its reasonable endeavours to obtain the Landlord's licence for the grant of the Underlease to the *Buyer* but shall not be required to commence proceedings for a declaration that consent is being unreasonably withheld.

F.5.3 The Underlease shall be on the same terms as the Overriding Lease but shall be granted for a term equal to the remainder of the term of the *Lease* plus three days or the longest period (less than three days) that will not wholly displace the Overriding Lease.]²

F.6 As soon as [either:—]

[F.6.1] the Overriding Lease and the licence to assign it to the *Buyer*[; or

F.6.2 the Overriding Lease and the licence to underlet to the *Buyer*]

have been granted to the *Seller* the *Seller* shall assign the Overriding Lease [or grant the Underlease (as the case may be)] to the *Buyer*.

F.7 The *Buyer* shall be liable for the *Seller's* reasonable costs in connection with the grant of the Overriding Lease (including the reasonable costs of the Landlord and stamp duty), the assignment of the Overriding Lease [or the grant of the Underlease (as the case may be)] and pending such assignment [or underletting] shall indemnify the *Seller* in respect of the costs (including rent) of all obligations under the Overriding Lease.

F.8 The *Buyer* may withdraw its request to the *Seller* to claim an Overriding Lease at any time before the grant of the Overriding Lease to the *Seller* and the *Buyer* shall be liable for the *Seller's* reasonable costs (including those of the Landlord) incurred in pursuance of the request down to the time of its withdrawal.

This clause enables the buyer of a lease subject to pre-1996 privity of contract rules to put in place safeguards which will only become relevant once he has ceased to be the tenant. The buyer can require the seller to obtain an overriding lease where a future tenant is in default, the seller having paid up and claimed against the buyer under the indemnity covenant. It is a buyer's amendment. Buyer's solicitors may also want to limit the indemnity covenants (whether express or implied by statute) so that the seller must make a claim within a limited period (say two months) of itself making a payment to the landlord (or earlier tenant), in order to avoid any danger that the time for claiming an overriding lease expires before the indemnity claim is made against the buyer.

This provision is a desirable, but not essential, widening of the rights under the Act which will benefit former tenants of old leases.

Include the provisions in both the contract and the transfer so that they can be located in the future if the contract is lost.

1. If the Seller obtained similar rights when it acquired the lease, consider passing requests for an overriding lease up the line in response to requests for indemnities passing down it.

2. Clauses F.5.2 and F.5.3 are only appropriate if the overriding lease will permit underletting.

Precedent 5: Contract clauses for sale of reversion subject to new leases

G.1 The *Seller* undertakes that [before][within the period of four weeks beginning with] the *Completion Date* it will serve notice on each of the tenants under the *Leases*[1] in accordance with section 8(1) of the Landlord and Tenant (Covenants) Act 1995 requesting complete release of the *Seller* from future liability under the landlord covenants contained in the *Leases*.

[G.2 If:—

G.2.1 more than [number or percentage] of the tenants under the *Leases* object and persist in objecting to the release of the *Seller*, and

G.2.2 the *Seller* obtains an opinion from counsel of not less than [10] years' call with experience in the field of landlord and tenant law that an application to the court for the release of the *Seller* has a [more than 50%] likelihood of success,

then the *Seller* shall apply to the court for a declaration that the release requested by the *Seller* is reasonable.]

G.3 The *Buyer* undertakes to supply promptly at the *Buyer's* cost such information as the *Seller* may [reasonably] require to satisfy any of the tenants under the *Leases* or the court that the release requested is reasonable and to act in good faith in respect of the provisions of this clause.

G.4 The *Seller* shall be under no obligation:—

G.4.1 to apply to the court if [number or percentage] or fewer of the tenants under the *Leases* object to the *Seller's* release; or

G.4.2 to appeal against the refusal of the court to declare that the release of the *Seller* is reasonable.

G.5 If at the *Completion Date* the *Seller* has not received consent (whether express or implied) for its release from all the landlord covenants contained in the *Leases* then the transfer shall contain the following provisions:—

'X With the object of affording to the *Seller* a full and sufficient indemnity but not further or otherwise the *Buyer* covenants with the *Seller* that, until such time (if ever) that the *Seller* is fully released from the landlord covenants of the *Leases*, the *Buyer* and its successors in title[2] will observe and perform all the landlord covenants contained in or referred to in the *Leases* and indemnify the *Seller* against all costs, claims, demands and proceedings in connection with any breach, non-observance or non-performance of such covenants.

Y Before the *Buyer* transfers the whole or any part of the *Property* which is subject to any of the *Leases* in respect of which the *Seller* remains unreleased:—

Y.1 the *Buyer* will notify the *Seller* so that the *Seller* has an opportunity to serve further notices under section 8(1) of the Landlord and Tenant (Covenants) Act 1995;

Y.2 the *Buyer* will obtain a covenant from its transferee with the *Seller* in the terms of this clause Y (including this sub-clause Y.2)

and the parties apply to the Chief Land Registrar to enter in the Proprietorship Register of the title to the *Property* a restriction preventing the registration of any transfer of the *Property* except under an Order of the Registrar unless the application for registration is accompanied by a certificate by the solicitors for the registered proprietor stating either that the provisions of this clause Y have been performed, or that the *Seller* has been completely released from future liability under the landlord covenants contained in the *Leases*.'

The only way to secure the indemnity included in this clause is for the seller to take a charge over the property. The practical difficulty with this solution is that it would prejudice the buyer's ability to finance (or refinance) the purchase.

1. It is assumed that all the leases to which the property is subject are new leases. However, there are likely to be many properties with a mixture of old and new leases, in which case this reference should be limited to the new leases.

2. The successors in title of the buyer of the reversion must be included in case the seller is not released on his own disposal or that of his immediate buyer. He has further opportunities to apply for release on each subsequent disposal, but this right is only of value if he receives timely warning of them.

Precedent 6: Contract clause for assignment of new lease where seller is giving or may give an AGA for the buyer[1]

If the *Landlord* requires the *Seller* to guarantee the performance by the *Buyer* of the tenant covenants in the *Lease*, the transfer or assignment shall contain the following provisions:—

'H LEASE INDEMNITY COVENANT

The *Buyer* covenants with the *Seller* that, with effect from the date of this deed until the *Buyer* is released from the tenant covenants of the *Lease* (including any period of statutory continuation of the tenancy created by the *Lease*), the *Buyer* and its successors in title[2] will:—

H.1 pay the rents reserved by and observe and perform the tenant covenants contained in the *Lease* and at all times indemnify the *Seller* against any non-payment, breach, non-performance or non-observance of such covenants and it is agreed and declared that no neglect or forbearance of the reversioner in endeavouring to obtain payment of such rents or of the *Seller* in endeavouring to enforce this covenant and no time or indulgence which may be given by the reversioner or the *Seller* shall in any way affect the liability of the *Buyer* under this covenant; and

H.2 procure that any person who shall take an assignment or transfer of the *Lease* from the *Buyer* in circumstances where the *Buyer* is not released from the tenant covenants of the *Lease* shall covenant by deed with the *Seller* in the same terms as the covenants set out in this clause and supply that deed 'to the *Seller* so that every future assignee or transferee of the *Lease* for whom the *Seller* may be liable under the guarantee shall have covenanted directly with the *Seller*.'

1. This clause can be adapted to cover the situation where an excluded assignment is made, rather than an immediate AGA. It will then be necessary to provide that the Buyer procures that on the assignment which ultimately releases the Seller, the assignee gives an indemnity in this form to the Seller in respect of any AGA which the Seller is required to give for that assignee.

2. The reference to successor in title is necessary, despite the abolition of continuing liability, in case the Buyer makes an excluded assignment in future.

Precedent 7: Clause for new lease limiting landlord's liability

I [X Ltd[1]] covenants as a personal obligation (but not so as to be liable after it shall have transferred all its estate and interest in the *Demised Premises* provided it has first complied with the provisions of clause I.1) in the terms set out in this clause I.

I.1 DIRECT COVENANTS BY ASSIGNEES OF THE REVERSION

I.1.1 to procure that any person to whom its estate and interest in the *Demised Premises* is to be transferred ('the Transferee') shall first covenant by deed with the *Tenant* in the same terms as set out in this clause I (including for the avoidance of doubt these sub-clauses I.1.1 and I.1.2) and supply that deed to the *Tenant* so that every future Transferee shall have covenanted directly with the *Tenant*; and

I.1.2 to apply to the Chief Land Registrar to enter in the Proprietorship Register of the *Landlord's* title to the *Demised Premises* a restriction preventing any transfer of the land comprised in that title except under an Order of the Registrar unless the application for registration is accompanied by a certificate by the solicitors for the registered proprietor that the Transferee has supplied to the *Tenant* a deed of covenant as required by clause I.1.1.

This is a landlord's amendment—although I.1.1 and I.1.2 benefit the tenant, they are part and parcel of the scheme for limiting the landlord's liability. It is thought that by making each landlord covenant in a personal capacity only his liability will be limited to the period when the lease is vested in him—see 2.4 of the text.

1. The first landlord should be named here, rather than using the defined term 'the Landlord'.